WAITING ON GOD

STRENGTH FOR TODAY AND
HOPE FOR TOMORROW

CHARLES F. STANLEY

HOWARD BOOKS
New York   Nashville   London   Toronto   Sydney   New Delhi

Howard Books
A Division of Simon & Schuster, Inc.
1230 Avenue of the Americas
New York, NY 10020

First Howard Books hardcover edition January 2015

HOWARD and colophon are trademarks of Simon & Schuster, Inc.

For information about special discounts for bulk purchases, please contact Simon & Schuster Special Sales at 1-866-506-1949 or business@simonandschuster.com.

The Simon & Schuster Speakers Bureau can bring authors to your live event. For more information or to book an event, contact the Simon & Schuster Speakers Bureau at 1-866-248-3049 or visit our website at www.simonspeakers.com.

Interior design by Renato Stanisic

Manufactured in the United States of America

10 9 8 7 6 5 4 3 2 1

Library of Congress Cataloging-in-Publication Data
Stanley, Charles F.
    Waiting on God : strength for today and hope for tomorrow / Charles F. Stanley.
        pages   cm
    Includes bibliographical references.
1. Trust in God—Christianity.   2. Expectation (Psychology)—Religious aspects—Christianity.   3. Waiting (Philosophy).   I. Title.
    BV4637.S733 2015
    248.4—dc23   2014034969

ISBN 978-1-4767-9403-7
ISBN 978-1-4767-9407-5 (ebook)

To all who wait—
that you will take heart and
continue to trust the One who never fails.

CONTENTS

WAITING ON GOD

Wait for the LORD;
be strong and let your heart take courage;
yes, wait for the LORD.
—Psalm 27:1

HOW LONG, O LORD?
A Look at the Long Road

Never.

It is the word that can stir the deepest fear in the bravest heart. *Never.*

"I'll never *find a job."*

"This will never *get better."*

"I'll never *be respected."*

"She will never *respond to me."*

"I'll never *get married."*

"I'll never *have the child I long for."*

"He will never *come home to me."*

It's the lie that originates with our sinful nature—it insists on putting a decisive end to all our hopes. *Don't bother to dream,* it whispers cruelly. *You don't deserve it. Stop wishing for what can* never *be.*

And so we continue to drive the nails into the coffin of our dearest longings.

"The Lord will never *answer my prayers."*

But this is the challenge of waiting on God. It's the ability to keep hoping when the *nevers* of life bombard us—when the minutes and hours, days and years, tick away without any answers to our most passionate pleas at the throne of grace. It's the faith to hang on to the Father on the long road, when human reason tells us to give up.

If the *nevers* of life are discouraging you, if you've waited for the Lord to fulfill His promises to you, if you wonder why God has allowed such a lengthy delay in answering the deepest cries of your heart—if this is where you are, friend—then this is the right book for you. There is meaning and hope in these times of waiting on the Lord to respond. Though you don't see Him working, you can know for certain that He is because He guarantees that He "acts on behalf of the one who waits for Him" (Isa. 64:4).

Not only that, but the Father has an awesome plan for you—purposes that are fantastic, perfectly suited for you, and that will give ultimate meaning to your life. However, God also has a very specific schedule—one that is often vastly different from what you'd expect. One that may have you wait far beyond what makes you comfortable. One that will most likely make you feel that all earthly hope is gone so that you will rely solely upon Him (2 Cor. 1:9).

What I intend to show you throughout these pages is that the only "never" you should focus on is that God will *never* let you down (Deut. 31:6, 8). So whatever it is you yearn for—no matter how long you

> The only *never* you should focus on is that God will *never* let you down.

have to wait—you can trust the Father to lead you and know for absolute certain that He has your very best interests in mind. The key for you is to remember *Whom* it is that you're really anticipating.

MY GRANDDAD'S LONG ROAD

That was certainly the case for my grandfather, George Washington Stanley. The first time I ever heard him preach was when I was nine years old—and to me, he looked like Moses because he seemed so very old and wise. He was tall, lanky, and he would get completely fired up whenever he proclaimed the gospel. I had no doubt that's what he was created to do. But I was surprised to discover that there was a time when he truly doubted he would ever be able to serve God.

You see, although Granddad knew the Lord had called him, churches in the area wouldn't allow him to fill their pulpits. One after another, they rejected him, causing him to doubt the calling he had received. Likewise, he felt very inadequate because he didn't have much education. In fact, he learned to read by studying the Bible. And he picked up how to preach by crying out to God and asking Him what to say.

A long time passed for Granddad with no open doors. One night, he became so distraught that he fell down on his knees on an unpaved road and cried out, "God, this seems impossible! If You're really calling me to preach and You're going to show me what to do, I need some evidence. Please, let me see a star fall." So he looked up and just about that time, one shot across the night sky like a blazing arrow.

But it wasn't enough. He was desperate—his fears went deep, the pressures overwhelming, and the memories of rejection were too real. So he said, "Lord, please, just one more time. Would You let me see one more falling star? Just to be sure?" Again he looked up. And again, a bright light rocketed across the celestial expanse.

He had his confirmation, but he still did not have a pulpit from which to speak. So he kept seeking God. After a time, the Lord showed him he could hold his revival meetings in a tent as others had done. So he did what any of us would do—he got a job to earn money so he could buy one.

Without much in the way of schooling and no training, he did the work that was available, which was as a tie hacker—someone who cut railroad ties for the local lines. He would chop down the trees, trim them to size, and earn twenty cents for each eight-foot tie he created, which was only a few each day.

There was a saying back then—and it was certainly true—that hacking ties was "a hard way to serve the Lord," even for turn-of-the-century laborers who were accustomed to putting their backs into their work. But my grandfather persevered, asking God to help him and staying open to His direction.

After several months of grueling labor and saving every penny, he had only forty dollars—a far cry from the three hundred dollars he needed to purchase the tent. Obviously, it would be a very long time before he could afford one. My grandfather told me that at that point he felt he'd *never* get around to preaching if he kept hacking ties.

> If God was calling him to preach, why was the road so long and so difficult?

I couldn't blame him for being discouraged. After all, if God was calling him to preach, why was the road so long, so filled with obstacles, and so difficult?

But Granddad didn't give up. Instead, he kept praying. "Lord, You called me to preach and know how much money I need for a tent. This is the best I can do, but I know You can help me. Father, please show me what to do."

Then one night, he was walking along a road and, again, was moved to his knees in prayer. But after he arose, he saw a house in the distance and knew that if he went there, God would provide for his needs. So Granddad went up to the house and knocked on the door, unsure of what he was supposed to say.

To his surprise, the lady who answered exclaimed, "Why Mr. Stanley! I've been wanting to talk to you. I have something for you." She invited him in and went to retrieve a small brown-paper sack. She handed it to him and said, "God told me to give you this." He thanked her, conversed with her for a while, and then left.

But when he opened the sack, he found three hundred one-dollar bills—exactly what he needed to purchase the tent. He told me that's when he learned to always trust God, pray to Him, wait for Him to work, and know for certain He will intervene.

The Lord used my grandfather in an awesome way because he obeyed Him and waited for His provision. In fact, Granddad didn't just preach, he went on to plant many churches in Virginia and North Carolina—including the church where I was saved in Danville, Virginia.

A NECESSITY

Did the Father use that time of waiting to teach my grandfather? Absolutely. Was it necessary for Granddad's spiritual growth? There is no doubt in my mind that it was.

Waiting is sometimes necessary for you and me as well. Learning to be directed by God's timing and wisdom—not our agenda—is one of the most important lessons we ever learn as believers. Of course, abiding by the Lord's schedule always takes faith and courage. But it is absolutely essential for living the Christian life, walking in obedience to the Father, and receiving the best of His blessings.

How do I know this? Because of all Scripture has to say about it.

- "O my God, in You I trust . . . Indeed, none of those who wait for You will be ashamed" (Ps. 25:2–3).
- "Wait for the LORD; be strong and let your heart take courage; yes, wait for the LORD" (Ps. 27:14).
- "Don't be impatient for the LORD to act! Keep traveling steadily along his pathway and in due season he will honor you with every blessing" (Ps. 37:34, TLB).
- "I waited patiently for the LORD; and He inclined to me and heard my cry. He brought me up out of the pit of destruction" (Ps. 40:1–2).
- "My soul, wait in silence for God only, for my hope is from Him. He only is my rock and my salvation, my stronghold; I shall not be shaken" (Ps. 62:5–6).
- "The LORD favors those who fear Him, those who wait for His lovingkindness" (Ps. 147:11).
- "The LORD longs to be gracious to you, and therefore He waits on high to have compassion on you. For the LORD is a God of justice; How blessed are all those who long for Him" (Isa. 30:18).
- "Those who wait for the LORD will gain new strength; they will mount up with wings like eagles, they will run and not get tired, they will walk and not become weary" (Isa. 40:31).

- "You will know that I am the LORD; those who hopefully wait for Me will not be put to shame" (Isa. 49:23).
- "From days of old they have not heard or perceived by ear, nor has the eye seen a God besides You, who acts in behalf of the one who waits for Him" (Isa. 64:4).
- "The LORD is good to those who wait for Him, to the person who seeks Him. It is good that he waits silently for the salvation of the LORD" (Lam. 3:25–26).
- "The vision is yet for the appointed time; it hastens toward the goal and it will not fail. Though it tarries, wait for it; for it will certainly come, it will not delay" (Hab. 2:3).
- "Hope that is seen is not hope; for who hopes for what he already sees? But if we hope for what we do not see, with perseverance we wait eagerly for it" (Rom. 8:24–25).

These are only a few of the verses, but you get the point. Time is one of God's most effective tools for teaching us to rely on Him. This has been true throughout history—seen often in the lives of the greatest saints such as Abraham, Joseph, and David. And it will be true until time itself is no more.

> Time is one of God's most effective tools for teaching us to rely upon Him.

WAITING ON GOD: A DEFINITION

Of course, no one *likes* delays. None of this diminishes the pain we feel as the days pass and we continue to struggle with our hopes and fears. Whether it's the hours that throw off our plans, caused by late planes and unyielding traffic jams; the days and weeks that cause us uncertainty, waiting for medical test results or decisions made by those outside our sphere of influence; or the years and decades we suffer through wondering if God will ever fulfill His promises—it is human to feel frustrated, anxious, and even as if our hopes are dying within us.

Why? Because we lack control over our circumstances. Someone else seems to be impeding our progress—deciding how the scant moments we've been given in this life will be spent and preventing us from enjoying the one thing we think will truly make us happy.

Like David we cry out, "How long, O LORD? Will You forget me forever? How long will You hide Your face from me? How long shall I take counsel in my soul, having sorrow in my heart all the day?" (Ps. 13:1–2).

Now, I don't know what it is you're hoping for, but I do know that you've picked up this book for a reason. I also know that waiting on God is one of the most difficult lessons to learn. I imagine that, like David, there is a lot of pain in your heart. You may fear the Lord has forgotten you or that He's found you undeserving of your dreams. Perhaps you feel rejected, confused, or even betrayed because He still hasn't given you what you've been trusting Him for. All the while, He is freely bestowing that job, that spouse, that child, that recognition, that promotion, that prosperity, or that blessing to people around you who don't even seem to realize or appreciate the amazing thing God has done for them.

You wonder, *Why not me? What makes me so unworthy?* Friend, I know it hurts more deeply than words can express. But please be assured, there is always hope with our heavenly Father.

So let's begin this journey with a definition of what it truly means to *wait on God*, because this will help clarify where our hearts and minds should be. We often make the mistake of thinking that His delays are just a waste of time—we do nothing, miss opportunities, and wish our lives away while He ignores us. However, that's not the case at all.

> Waiting on God is one of the most difficult lessons you and I will ever learn.

First, the Lord is not neglecting you and has not forgotten you.

Your heavenly Father is working in the unseen on your behalf (Isa. 64:4)—every single moment. You may not perceive Him, and you could not possibly conceive how He is working out everything for you

(Eph. 3:20–21)—nor would you understand it all if you saw it. This is by design so you will honor Him as God and abandon yourself to His care. Your responsibility is to set your heart on Him and trust that your life is safe in His all-powerful, wise, and loving hands.

Second, you are not just waiting around, doing nothing.

> Your responsibility is to set your heart on Him and trust that your life is safe in His all-powerful, wise, and loving hands.

People who anticipate the Father's instruction and intervention should continue serving Him and carrying out their daily business. You must keep seeking, obeying, and having intimate fellowship with Him. You must persist in building your relationship with Him, even when circumstances don't seem to be going your way.

Third, you are not missing worthwhile opportunities.

It may seem as if you are. It may truly appear as if there is no better option on the horizon for you. But if God says, "No" or "Wait" about some possibility before you, trust Him. Don't try to "make it happen." Rather, count on His faultless wisdom to protect you from choices that would ultimately harm you.

Fourth, you are not alone.

Everyone you know is facing a delay in some area or another. Yes, you may look around and see people enjoying the blessing you desire. You may think you are the only one struggling with your particular issue—the only one the Father has not provided for. And such thoughts may stir up feelings of shame, disappointment, and despair because you wonder what's wrong with you. But friend, realize that those thoughts of humiliation and defeat come from your enemy, who is always trying to isolate and destroy you.

First Peter 5:8–9 reminds you, "Your adversary, the devil, prowls around like a roaring lion, seeking someone to devour. But resist him, firm in your faith, knowing that the same experiences of suffering are being accomplished by your brethren who are in the world." In every nation, there are people just like you, waiting for similar blessings and experiencing the same feelings. In fact, throughout Scripture, you cannot find a man or woman whom God used in a powerful way who did not first face a long and difficult time of waiting. So do not despair. Rather, take it as the Father's special favor and guidance in your life.

What we can draw from all this is that waiting on the Lord signifies an expectant endurance that is demonstrated by a *directed*, *purposeful*, *active*, and *courageous* attitude of prayer. Let's take a closer look at this. *Expectant endurance* is exhibited in this way:

- *Directed*—Rather than concentrating on what we're waiting for, we persevere with expectant endurance when we *focus on the Father*, whom we know has the best plan for our lives.
- *Purposeful*—As we practice expectant endurance, we find meaning in the delay because we look *with anticipation* for God's perfect direction, preparation, and provision.
- *Active*—As we wait with expectant endurance, we trust that the Lord is working in the unseen; thus, as we discover His will, we claim His promises and continue obeying Him step-by-step.
- *Courageous*—Expectant endurance also means we are willing to face adversity and forgo *good* opportunities in order to take hold of the Lord's very *best* for our lives.

DAVID'S LONG ROAD

In other words, we don't become impatient—making our own way or running ahead of the Lord's plan. Instead, we are patient, optimistic, and hopeful. We remain in our present circumstances until we receive further instructions and His intervention. This is never easy, of course. But I—along with many whose lives have impacted God's kingdom— can testify that the Father makes our wait worthwhile.

Throughout this book, we will discuss the *directed, purposeful, active,* and *courageous* aspects of waiting on the Lord. But let's take a minute now to look at the life of David and discover the valuable principles the Father teaches us as we wait upon Him. Like many of us, David went through some very long and perplexing trials. In fact, if anyone had a right to be confused and disappointed about how life was turning out, it was David.

_____

Waiting on God
means remaining
in your present
circumstances until
you receive further
instructions and
His intervention.

_____

First Samuel 16 tells us that David was a mere teenager—probably around sixteen— when the prophet Samuel anointed him to succeed Saul as king of Israel (v. 13). At first, everything seemed to be going very well. Almost immediately, the Lord provided a way for David to become an important figure in Saul's court, making him the king's personal musician and armor bearer. Saul proclaimed, "Let David now stand before me, for he has found favor in my sight" (v. 22), and Scripture testifies that "Saul loved him greatly" (v. 21).

Likewise, David had many great successes in those early years. He beat the mighty Philistine warrior-giant Goliath (1 Sam. 17), which proved him to be a worthy soldier. He became like a brother to Saul's firstborn son, Jonathan (1 Sam. 18:1–3). He was promoted to a high rank in the army because of his many victories (1 Sam. 18:5, 14, 30). He married Saul's daughter, princess Michal (1 Sam. 18:27). And David was absolutely loved by all of Israel (1 Sam. 18:16). Life seemed to be right on track for the fulfillment of God's promise.

At this point, I wonder what David thought about. No doubt, he dreamt about how the Lord would give him the kingdom, as any person in his position would. Both Saul and Israel adored him, after all, and the Father had promised David the throne. Perhaps he envisioned a dying Saul calling him to his side and quietly transferring power. Or maybe he prayed Saul would just humbly step aside someday, happily acknowledging that God had anointed David to be monarch. Scripture doesn't say what hopes were hidden in this young man's heart.

What we do know, however, is that one day, all of David's circumstances changed dramatically—and not for the better. We're told, "When Saul saw and knew that the LORD was with David . . . Saul was even more afraid of David. Thus Saul was David's enemy continually. . . . Saul told Jonathan his son and all his servants to put David to death" (1 Sam. 18:28–29, 19:1).

And just like that, David's life took a radical turn for the worse. For years, he struggled with devastating losses, attempts on his life, demoralizing injustices, and excruciating heartaches (1 Sam. 19–30). Instead of enjoying life in the kingdom he'd been promised, he was eventually forced to flee from Israel altogether. And 1 Samuel 23:14 (TLB) reports, "Saul hunted him day after day, but the LORD didn't let him find him."

You can imagine the absolute hopelessness and rejection David felt. He had been so close to having his heart's desire. Not only was the fulfillment of his dreams further away than ever, but overwhelming problems mounted against him even though he was trying to do everything right. Saul sought to destroy David and persecuted anyone who tried to help him. The very friends he'd fought next to as a military commander now sought to execute him. He was far from his home and loved ones. He continually faced attacks from enemy armies and was forced to seek shelter in foreign lands. Under such circumstances, David must have wondered if he would even live to be king.

And to add insult to injury, Saul was acting in an extremely ungodly manner—viciously killing the innocent priests and people of Nob (1 Sam. 22:6–19) and sinfully consulting the witch of Endor (1 Sam. 28:5–20). Why was the Lord tolerating Saul's wickedness?

David was a person just like you and me—with physical limitations, failings, emotions, fears, and dreams—and he faced many of the same pressures and heartbreaks you and I experience every day. Read that last sentence again. Really think about what David had to endure. Of course, not many of us will understand the terrible stress of someone seeking to assassinate us or having to flee to another nation for safety as David did. But we know what it is to have enemies, to be targeted unfairly, to be despised as outcasts, to have our hopes crushed, to have our security stripped away, to foresee only bleak and uncertain futures, to watch the wicked seemingly flourish as we despair, to feel utterly alone, and to wonder where the Lord is in our situation.

Of course, finding himself in such a disheartening condition, David could have questioned the discipline he was experiencing—as many of us would. He could have been tempted to call the Lord unjust. He could have said, "God promised I would be king. I should raise an army and take the throne from that evil Saul." He could have taken matters into his own hands. But he didn't.

Instead, he kept seeking and obeying the Lord. In fact, David had two opportunities to kill Saul (1 Sam. 24; 26), and he refused to take them, saying, "Far be it from me because of the LORD that I should do this thing to my lord, the LORD's anointed, to stretch out my hand against him, since he is the LORD's anointed" (1 Sam. 24:6). He demonstrated beyond a shadow of a doubt that he honored God's timing above all else.

This doesn't mean David didn't struggle. In fact, he did—terribly. He wrote, "I would have despaired unless I had believed that I would see the goodness of the LORD in the land of the living" (Ps. 27:13). As I said, he felt all the same pain and anxiety we do. And if he hadn't had the Father to hold on to, he would have been absolutely devastated.

> "I would have despaired unless I had believed that I would see the goodness of the LORD in the land of the living" (Ps. 27:13).

But because David strengthened himself in the Lord, he was able to make it through—clinging to the hope of a better day ahead and willing to learn all God was teaching him. This is why he was able to counsel, "Wait for the LORD; be strong and let your heart take courage; yes, wait for the LORD" (Ps. 27:14).

So what did David discover in the delays? Why was it wise for him to wait for the Lord? And why is it important for you? What lessons did David learn while he expectantly waited on God?

1. TO ACCEPT GOD'S DIRECTION

First, David learned how important it is to listen to the Father and receive His clear direction. The Lord separated David from the king's court and from his friends so he would have only one place to go for counsel—to the all-knowing God of creation, who is perfect in His wisdom, understanding, and insight.

Do not ever underestimate how absolutely crucial this is. You see, whenever we come to important decisions in our lives, we often go to our earthly sources of guidance—our friends, advisors, and even the Internet. But these sources are extremely limited and often very faulty places to receive assistance. However, when we trust Jesus as our Savior, we have a much more informed and effective Source of instruction and direction, who provides everything we need as we obey Him. And in order to receive the very best He has for our lives, we must listen to what He says.

We can see the importance of seeking God's guidance when David finally became ruler over all Israel and the Philistines engaged in two campaigns against him (2 Sam. 5). Of course, the Philistines had been enemies of Israel for almost two centuries—since the time of the judges (Judg. 3:31)—and had been responsible for the death of Saul (1 Sam. 31:1–6). So when King David conquered the city of Jerusalem and made it his capital, they took the opportunity to attack. And David did what he had been accustomed to doing; he asked God how to proceed.

Second Samuel 5:19 reports, "David inquired of the Lord, saying, 'Shall I go up against the Philistines? Will You give them into my hand?' And the Lord said to David, 'Go up, for I will certainly give the Philistines into your hand.' " It shouldn't surprise anyone to discover that David quickly claimed the victory.

However, when the Philistines gathered for a second time in the Valley of Rephaim, they came with reinforcements—the historian Josephus reported, "with an army three times as numerous as before" (*Antiquities of the Jews* VII, 4:1). So when David asked God what to do, the Lord changed His instructions. "He said, 'You shall not go directly up; circle around behind them and come at them in front of the balsam trees. It shall be, when you hear the sound of marching in the tops of the balsam trees, then you shall act promptly, for then the LORD will have gone out before you to strike the army of the Philistines' " (2 Sam. 5:23–24).

In other words, instead of standing between the Philistines and Jerusalem and attacking the enemy army from the front as they were accustomed, the Israeli troops were to move around to the outside of the Philistine camp—where the enemy wouldn't expect them to be—and wait for them to flee.

Militarily, this made no sense, of course. No earthly general or strategist would have suggested this. But David trusted God and patiently awaited His march across the tops of the trees. And the Lord Himself drove the Philistines out from the Rephaim Valley, allowing David to pursue the enemy all the way back to their border. This victory ultimately secured Jerusalem, and 1 Chronicles 14:17 reports, "The fame of David went out into all the lands; and the LORD brought the fear of him on all the nations."

Likewise, you need to learn that even when the Father's instruction seems unreasonable or illogical, His plans are good, right, and in your best interests (Prov. 3:5–6). And waiting on Him teaches you how to avoid operating by the world's limited perception of your circumstances and how to rely upon His far wiser, supernatural, powerful plan. So when you cannot see your way clear, stay where you are until God answers you and trust Him to teach you the way you should go.

> When you cannot see your way clear, stay where you are until God answers you and trust Him to teach you the way you should go.

2. TO VALUE GOD'S TIMING

The second lesson David learned was the importance of walking in step with the Lord's schedule. In other words, he realized that time was a tool God was using to effectively carry out His will and build dedication to His plan in David's life and throughout Israel.

Perhaps the best example of this was exhibited in the two opportunities David had to execute Saul (1 Sam. 24; 26). Both times, David's men urged him to kill Saul, and we can only imagine the pressure David felt to take matters into his hands. How would *not* killing Saul look to those who faithfully followed him? Would they understand his dedication to God? Would they tolerate more months and years on the run from Saul's forces? Or would they abandon him—thinking him too cowardly to take the kingdom promised to him?

David could have been driven by what others thought. But he wasn't. He did not dwell on Saul's harshness toward him or how to maintain popular support. Rather, he was patient and determined to wait until the Lord gave him the kingdom—seeking wholeheartedly to serve God rather than man.

He said in faith, "As the LORD lives, surely the LORD will strike him, or his day will come that he dies, or he will go down into battle and perish. The LORD forbid that I should stretch out my hand against the LORD's anointed" (1 Sam. 26:11). David knew God would take care of the situation in His perfect time. So he did not need to wrestle with his circumstances, make a way for himself, or figure out how to turn the situation to his advantage. He simply waited for direction from the Father.

And because he did, the Lord blessed David with great support and cleared the way for him to become king—just as He had said He would (2 Sam. 5).

You see, what we desire is often what the Lord has purposed and will provide for us. But timing is everything, and key puzzle pieces are falling into place as we wait. God is changing hearts and engineering circumstances we have no idea even exist. Therefore, the delays we face are not a denial of His promises; rather, they are an integral part of His strategy to arrange all the details and get us positioned for His excellent plan.

Therefore, when the pressure is on and everything around you is pushing you to move, move, move, and God says, "Don't even think about budging"—listen to Him. Like David, stay where you are and trust Him to work on your behalf. Do so with the understanding that when you run ahead of Him—taking matters into your own hands or forcing your way into opportunities you have no business partaking of—you undermine and even destroy the good things He's designed for you. But when you accept His schedule, you know for certain you will receive His very best blessings.

3. TO PREPARE FOR HIS BLESSINGS

Third, as David waited for the promise to be fulfilled, God was preparing him to be the godly, wise ruler Israel needed.

This doesn't mean David never faltered or failed as king—we know he did. But through it all, the Lord "testified and said, 'I HAVE FOUND DAVID the son of Jesse, A MAN AFTER MY HEART, who will do all My will' " (Acts 13:22).

Likewise, the Father does not expect you to be faultless. That is why He sent Jesus to be your sinless, all-sufficient Savior—to justify you and be perfect for you. But the Father takes every opportunity to prepare you for His blessing so you can enjoy it fully.

As I stated before, many times what you most desire is what God wants for you as well. However, the gift that would be completely wonderful for you tomorrow may be absolutely destructive to you today. So He lingers, develops you, and matures your character so that you are fully equipped to receive all He has planned for you.

> God lingers, develops you, and matures your character so that you are fully equipped to receive all He has planned for you.

For example, when my son Andy was just a small boy—around three or four years old—he saw my pocketknife and was absolutely fascinated by it. He asked me to give him one. Although it was a gift I would eventually provide, I realized how unwise it would be to hand such a potentially dangerous tool to such a young child—he just wasn't ready. And I loved Andy far too much to endanger him that way. But when he was mature enough to handle it, I was glad to buy him the pocketknife he wanted. In the same way, the

Father waits until we grow spiritually so that the blessings He's planned do not harm us, but are a source of great joy to us.

But there is a second way the Lord prepares us. Not only does He cultivate your character for protection, but He also does so to increase your commitment. I've experienced this principle throughout my life. The greater the blessing, the longer God will have you tarry, in order to fortify your resolve to glorify Him with it.

You see, every gift comes with responsibilities and challenges. Whether you desire a particular occupation, relationship, ministry, or what have you, when the difficult times arrive and you are in the thick of battle, you may be tempted to run. But if you wait on God for that blessing, you will never forget the process of attaining your heart's desire. In fact, you will treasure it more and seek to honor Him as you nurture and care for it. You won't question whether you made the right decision. You will refuse to let go of it regardless of how hot the fire, how deep the water, how black the storm clouds, or how thick the fog. Rather, your heart will be absolutely set to trust the Lord no matter your circumstances.

> The greater the blessing, the longer God will have you tarry, in order to fortify your resolve to glorify Him with it.

4. TO STRENGTHEN OUR FAITH

The fourth benefit David received from this waiting time was that his faith grew greatly. Why? Because you cannot wait upon God without learning to truly trust Him. And you cannot exercise your hope in Him if you are always given everything immediately (Rom. 8:24–25). But when we have only His promise to rely upon—with absolutely no visible evidence of answered prayer—then our faith is put to the test and can grow (2 Cor. 5:7).

For this purpose, the Lord will *intentionally* put adverse conditions in our path so we will choose to believe Him rather than focus on our circumstances—which is what usually gets us in the most trouble.

We know from Scripture that David had to remind himself of God's promises and renew his faith in the Lord often because of the adversity he was experiencing. Psalm 57 chronicles his lament as he fled from Saul to En Gedi. You can imagine his loneliness, fear, and dejection as he laid his head on a rock in a dark cave—rather than on a pillow in a palace—knowing that his life was in imminent danger. David wrote, "My soul is among lions; I must lie among those who breathe forth fire, even the sons of men, whose teeth are spears and arrows and their tongue a sharp sword" (v. 4). Alone, in peril, pursued by those who sought to execute him—how could he possibly hope to be king? Too many obstacles remained in his path. It seemed impossible.

But David intentionally set his focus on God and expressed his faith:

> Be gracious to me, O God, be gracious to me,
> For my soul takes refuge in You;
> And in the shadow of Your wings I will take refuge
> Until destruction passes by.
> I will cry to God Most High,
> To God who accomplishes all things for me.
> He will send from heaven and save me;
> He reproaches him who tramples upon me. Selah.
> God will send forth His lovingkindness and His truth.
> (vv. 1–3, emphasis added)

David fixed his thoughts on the Father's faithfulness rather than his trials, and he remained certain that the Lord would fulfill all He had promised (v. 2). In that way, his faith was strengthened.

Likewise, any time you choose to trust God even when circumstances appear contrary, you are exercising and establishing your faith.

I've had many times in my life when the Lord spoke to my heart about what He was going to do. But then, as troubling obstacles and challenges arose, I would look around and think, "How in the world can this happen?" Then the Lord would say to me, "Are you going to believe what you see or will you trust Me?" So, as difficult as it was, I would make the decision to "walk by faith, not by sight" (2 Cor. 5:7). And I am so glad I did! Because each and every time, I was blessed to experience the Father's astounding presence and provision (Heb. 10:35–39).

Friend, I can say without a shadow of a doubt that you will never go wrong waiting on God. You will never be disappointed when you trust Him to make a way for you regardless of how your circumstances may appear. And when you make the choice to believe Him, He will grow your faith in awesome ways.

> I can say without a shadow of a doubt that you will never go wrong waiting on God.

5. TO SIFT OUR MOTIVES AND DESIRES

Of course, one of the most important reasons God allows us to experience seasons of waiting is to sift our motives. Why is it that we feel such distress when we are denied our heart's desire? Is it because we love it more than the Father? Are we somehow avoiding obedience or seeking to replace Him with something or someone else? Is there some sin the Lord is seeking to purge from our lives before He answers our prayers?

Your request may be well within God's will for you, but if your motives are wrong or your tactics are sinful, He will work to align your heart with His purposes. This is not to punish you; rather, this is for your good—so that you can experience the greater freedom, more meaningful success, and deeper joy that are found only in Him.

Certainly David witnessed the dangers of seeking anything other than the Lord by observing King Saul, whose jealous desire for power destroyed him. The question was constantly before each of them: *As king, will you remain submitted as a servant of the Lord? Or do you seek to make God serve you? Will you rule Israel on His behalf or for yourself?*

Saul made his choice—which was to seek after his own agenda and glory rather than God's (1 Sam. 15). And because of it, he lost everything. Samuel informed Saul, "Because you have rejected the word of the LORD, He has also rejected you from being king . . . The LORD has torn the kingdom of Israel from you today and has given it to your neighbor, who is better than you" (1 Sam. 15:23, 28).

On the other hand, God took a great deal of time to sift and purify David's heart. And David proclaimed his choice in Psalm 86:12, "I will give thanks to You, O LORD my God, with all my heart, and will glorify Your name forever." He learned that there is a vast difference between genuinely seeking the Father and merely pursuing His gifts, intervention, and benefits. And because he chose to serve God wholeheartedly, the Lord accomplished many astounding achievements through David.

First, "the LORD gave him victories wherever he turned" (2 Sam. 8:6, TLB)—no other king gained as much territory for Israel as David did. Not only did he conquer the exceedingly important city of Jerusalem (2 Sam. 5:6–10), but God also worked through David to fulfill His covenant to Abraham: "To your descendants I have given this land, from the river of Egypt as far as the great river, the river Euphrates" (Gen. 15:18).

Second, the Father promised David, "Your house and your kingdom shall endure before Me forever; your throne shall be established forever" (2 Sam. 7:16). Whereas Saul's kingdom had been torn from him, David's would be eternal. How? Through the Messiah—the Lord Jesus our Savior, who was often called "the Son of David" in the New Testament (such as in Matt. 1:1; 9:27; and 21:9—to name a few).

Finally, God allowed David's profound, comforting, and beautiful words in the psalms to become part of the enduring canon of Scripture. How many of us throughout the years have been consoled, instructed, and encouraged because of his faithful testimony?

The truth of the matter is that our goals are generally very small and unsatisfying compared to the awesome, eternal plans the Father desires to accomplish through us. So what I would like you to see here is that when God allows us to wait, it is for our good. If we—like Saul—are only focused on what the Father can do for us, we've missed the point of having a relationship with Him. We exist for *His* glory—not the other way around. But if He sifts us as He did David, then there is no telling what wonderful, exciting, energizing, and fulfilling things He's purposed to do through us. As Jesus said, "I chose you and appointed you so that you might go and bear fruit—*fruit that will last*—and so that whatever you ask in my name the Father will give you" (John 15:16, NIV, emphasis added).

Of course, this is a constant struggle we all face—the challenge to keep God on the throne of our hearts instead of ourselves. It is so easy to become absorbed in our own concerns that we forget that we belong to Him. But nothing teaches us so effectively as a prolonged difficulty. Unable to handle it on our own, we turn to Him out of desperation and ultimately realize how truly loving, wise, and good He really is.

NEVER GIVE UP

The fourth president of Wheaton College, Victor Raymond Edman, summed up the discipline of waiting in David's life like this, "The delay seemed to be interminable and intolerable, but was indispensable in preparing David for his long career as king of his people, to which office he had been appointed many years before. Delay never thwarts God's purpose; rather, it polishes His instrument." You can be certain the same is true for you—in your waiting, the Father is refining you and fitting you for His awesome purposes.

> "Delay never thwarts God's purpose; rather, it polishes His instrument."
>
> —Victor Raymond Edman

Dear friend, are you unsure of your way? Do you have needs only He can provide? Is your path blocked on every side? Do you wonder if God has forgotten you? The *nevers* of life can discourage you and rend your heart if you don't focus on the One who ultimately holds your future in His hands.

Your heavenly Father isn't driven, limited, or intimidated by seeming impossibilities or complex earthly circumstances. Rather, He is motivated to act on your behalf out of His unconditional love and the wonderful plans He has for you. He is working powerfully to teach you to listen to Him, transform your character, strengthen your commitment, establish your faith, and free you from bondage. And in the next chapter we will look at the reasons you can trust Him to do so.

Therefore, don't despair and never give up! This season of waiting is for an excellent purpose. And if you will remain in your present circumstances until you receive further instructions—seeking His face, obeying Him, and walking by faith rather than sight—you will certainly not be disappointed.

Father, how very grateful I am that these times of waiting are not in vain, but are meant for Your good purposes. Thank You for being so intimately involved in my life and for teaching me how important it is to wait on You.

Lord Jesus, I confess that when there are difficult circumstances, the pain can reach deep, the pressure can crush, and the anxiety can overwhelm me. At times I feel trapped without recourse—imprisoned, chained, and without hope.

But Father, I thank You that with You there is always hope! And even right now I express my faith that You can and will help me in the situations that are heavy on my heart. Lord, please reveal to me how You are acting on my behalf and what You desire for me to learn through this trial. Garrison me about with Your loving, powerful presence, peace, and assurance. Teach me what it means to sit expectantly before You in an attitude of directed, purposeful, active, and courageous prayer. And in all things, help me to seek Your face, obey Your commands, reflect Your character, act in faith, and have pure motives that honor You.

Thank You for this time of waiting, Father. It is difficult to say that, but I know You are working all things for my good and I will see the fulfillment of Your promises if I cling to You. To You be all the glory and praise. In Jesus' holy and wonderful name I pray. Amen.

POINTS FOR ACTIVE WAITING

1. Memorize Psalm 27:14: "Wait for the LORD; be strong and let your heart take courage; yes, wait for the LORD."

2. Whenever you feel anxious or sorrowful because of what you are waiting for, repeat Psalm 27:14 to yourself.

3. Review the five reasons God may have you wait (beginning on page 13). Do any of them stand out? Is the Father speaking to you about any of these issues? If so, write them down in the space provided or in your journal and remind yourself about them as often as necessary. It is important to remember that you are making progress in these areas.

4. Spend time in *directed, purposeful, active,* and *courageous* prayer daily, asking the Father what He is teaching you. In your journal or in the space provided, record the Scripture verses and principles He brings to mind and encourage yourself with them. You may have to do this often. But you honor the Lord by clinging to Him during the delays.

5. Whenever you grow discouraged, remember to thank God for His activity in the unseen (Isa. 64:4). Why? Because refocusing your attention from your circumstances to His ability to help you will always encourage your soul. You are promised in Psalm 50:23, "He who offers a sacrifice of thanksgiving honors Me; and to him who orders his way aright I shall show the salvation of God." Take time to write a prayer of thanksgiving in the space provided.

Use this space to respond to the "Points for Active Waiting" and to record prayer requests, key lessons God is teaching you, and your insights about waiting on the Lord to act on your behalf.

My soul, wait in silence for God only,
for my hope is from Him.
He only is my rock and my salvation, my stronhold;
I shall not be shaken.
—Psalm 62:5–6

{ 2 }

ASSURED IN GOD'S CHARACTER
The Wisdom of Directing Your Focus to Him

Do you know *who* it is you are waiting for? Someone may say, "Well, I am hoping for an employer to notice my résumé." Another person might add, "I am awaiting a spouse," or, "I am anticipating having a child." We tend to focus on the object of our desire rather than the Provider. But really—no matter what the subject of your petitions—the One you are actually waiting for is God. You are hoping He will answer your prayers. You are expecting Him to supply the solution to your problem. You are awaiting His intervention. After all, the reality is, "Every good thing given and every perfect gift is from above, coming down from the Father of lights, with whom there is no variation or shifting shadow" (James 1:17). It is the Lord Himself who provides all things for you.

This was the case for the primitive Lahu people of northeastern Myanmar. It was the late 1800s, the land was still called Burma, and the people wore ropes on their wrists symbolizing their "bondage to evil spirits."[1] Yet they knew someone would appear who would tell them about the One who could deliver them. And they understood that the messenger would bring them the Book of the One True God—whom they called *Gui'Sha*, which means "the Creator of all things."[2] Author and pastor Hal Seed explains, "The Lahu believed they could not fully obey Gui'Sha's laws until they regained the precise written form of his laws. Their holy men taught that when the right time came, Gui'Sha would send a white brother with a white book containing the laws of Gui'Sha."

One day, as they made the long journey from their mountain village to sell their goods at the market in Kengtung, they noticed an odd-looking man explaining the Ten Commandments. In his book *Eternity in Their Hearts*, missionary Don Richardson described the scene: "They stared incredulously at his white face, the white interior of the book in his hand, and listened to his description—in the Shan language—of the laws of God contained in that book." Instantly they knew this was the brother they had been expecting. They told the missionary, "We as a people have been waiting for you for centuries. . . . We even have meeting houses built in some of our villages in readiness for your coming."[3]

Of course, William Marcus Young had no idea about how God would use him to reach the Lahu when he left America in 1892 and set out to evangelize the Shan people of Kengtung, Burma. He simply obeyed the Lord and preached the gospel. And really, the Lahu people had not been waiting centuries for *him*—Young could do nothing to release them from the sins that held them in bondage. Rather, they were yearning for the salvation only Jesus offers. They were looking expectantly for God.

> "We . . . have been waiting for you."

And whether you realize it or not, friend—so are you.

A CHANGE OF FOCUS

Just as God orchestrated the events in William Marcus Young's life to meet the needs of the Lahu people, He is arranging unseen circumstances to answer your prayers as well.

This is why one of my main goals in this book is to help you change your focus from the gift to the Giver—from the blessing to the One who bestows it. Ultimately, it is "God who accomplishes all things for" you (Ps. 57:2)—just as He did for the Lahu people, David, and my granddad.

Remember what we discussed in Chapter 1: waiting signifies an expectant endurance that is demonstrated by a *directed, purposeful, active,* and *courageous* attitude of prayer. That expectant endurance means we won't make a move without the Lord's guidance. And that first characteristic of godly prayer in waiting—being *directed toward God*—is what we'll be examining in this chapter. Rather than concentrating on what we're waiting for, we *focus on the Father,* who has the best plan for our lives.

Of course, you may say, "Focus on God? You just don't understand how desperately I want to have a baby. I can't seem to stop thinking about it." I understand how difficult it may appear to shift your thoughts to Him,

> Change your focus from the gift to the Giver—from the blessing to the One who bestows it.

but I can say without a shadow of a doubt that with the help and power of the Holy Spirit and some godly biblical principles to live by, you can do it. And I can absolutely assure you that you will be a more fulfilled individual and a better mother if you center your attention on the Father, who accomplishes all things for you (Ps. 138:8).

Or maybe you are thinking, "I have real bills to pay—I need a job." But I would remind you of Philippians 4:19, "My God will supply all your needs according to His riches in glory in Christ Jesus." I would also direct you to Deuteronomy 8:18, which instructs, "You shall remember the LORD your God, for it is He who is giving you power to make wealth." If you are not seeking and obeying the Father, you may be missing the ways He is sustaining you and the vital blessings He is summoning you to take hold of. No, He may not provide for you in the manner you expect, but He will never forsake the person who seeks Him (Ps. 9:10).

In fact, no matter what you are waiting for, ultimately, you are better prepared and suited for it if you are centered on God. Why? Because when you focus on what you lack, it inspires despair in your heart. You obsess over your own limitations, which reinforces the bondage within you. Remember, you sin when you try to meet your needs in your way

rather than the Lord's. So as you fixate on what you don't have, you en-
slave yourself more to the sin nature, which eventually leads to destruction (Rom. 6:23). It is a disheartening and vicious cycle.

But when you single-mindedly set your sights on God, you realize the
incredible strength, wisdom, and power that are being employed on your
behalf. You have confidence because the Lord knows and provides what
is absolutely best for you. And because He is unaffected by the obstacles
that limit and intimidate you, your reasons to fear disappear (Isa. 41:10).

Friend, the Lord God is *faithful*. If He makes a promise, He will
certainly keep it. Don't miss this principle, because it is one of the
most important lessons you can ever learn about your ability to wait on
Him—*it is based completely on your understanding of who He is and your
relationship with Him.*

DO YOU REALLY KNOW HIM?

Therefore, let us start at the beginning point of knowing Him with this
simple question: *Have you accepted Jesus as your Lord and Savior?*

Have you ever experienced the wonderful forgiveness of all your
sins and the life-changing blessing of a restored relationship with the
Father? I ask this because if you haven't, you will not be able to trust
Him. So much of your capacity to remain faithful during waiting times
is the work of the Holy Spirit, who reminds you of what God has promised you and how trustworthy He is (John 14:26). However, the Holy
Spirit does not come to dwell in you until you receive Jesus as your Lord
and Savior. He is your assurance that your eternal relationship with God
is real (Eph. 1:13–14).

So here is my challenge to you. Spend a few minutes thinking about
what your last moments in this life will be like. Perhaps you are lying
on a bed in a hospital or in your home. One after another, the machines
monitoring your vitals indicate that your organs are shutting down.
Your temperature and blood pressure drop. Your heart rate slows.
Your breathing becomes shallow and irregular. You find it increasingly

difficult to engage with your surroundings. Finally, you are struck with the realization that this is it—in a few moments, the life that you know will be over. Close your eyes and let that sink in.

How do you feel? What emotions do thoughts such as these stir up within you?

Do you begin to panic—overcome by anxiety? Are you scared—uncertain as to what will happen? Does the sharp pain of regret pierce your heart?

Or do feelings of peace and joy flood your soul because you are about to see your beloved Savior face-to-face?

The Holy Spirit is speaking to you right now through the emotions you're experiencing. Remember, His fruit is "love, joy, peace, patience, kindness, goodness, faithfulness, gentleness, [and] self-control" (Gal. 5:22–23). If your thoughts of meeting the Lord are characterized by these traits, you know He is working powerfully within you. But if your attitude about facing Him is marked with confusion, apathy, anger, pain, regret, or overwhelming fear, then either you do not know Him as well as you should or you may not know Jesus at all. And if you can't trust Him completely with your salvation, then it will be impossible for you to truly rely on Him through life's delays.

But you don't have to wrestle with uncertainty. There is no need to suffer with anxiety as you think about your last moments here on earth. You can know for sure that the end of this existence means the beginning of an even better life—eternal life with Him in heaven (2 Cor. 5:1–8). You can have inexpressible joy and the "the peace of God, which surpasses all comprehension" (Phil. 4:7).

How? By realizing that as your Savior, Jesus pays your sin debt *in full* (Rom. 6:23). Your sin is what separates you from God (Isa. 59:2). But when you accept the salvation Christ has provided for you on the Cross, He forgives your transgressions, reconciles you to the Father, and gives you His permanent and unfailing holiness (Rom. 5). You cannot earn it (Gal. 2:16), and you cannot possibly lose it (John 10:27–30). All He asks is that you accept it by faith (John 3:16–18).

So how do you take hold of this wonderful gift of salvation that Christ offers you? Romans 10:9–10 instructs: "If you confess with your mouth Jesus as Lord, and believe in your heart that God raised Him from the dead, you will be saved; for with the heart a person believes, resulting in righteousness, and with the mouth he confesses, resulting in salvation."

Therefore, if you have never asked Jesus to be your Lord and Savior, I invite you to do so right now. You can tell Him in your own words or use this simple prayer:

> *Lord Jesus, I come to You asking You to forgive my sins and save me from eternal separation from God. In faith, I accept Your work and death on the Cross as sufficient payment for my transgressions. I also confess that You are Lord. Help me to turn from my sins and live in a manner that is pleasing to You.*
>
> *I praise You for providing the way for me to know You and to have a relationship with my heavenly Father. Through faith in You, I have eternal life and no longer have any reason to fear death. You have conquered the grave, Lord Jesus, and I trust You have prepared a home in heaven for me.*
>
> *Thank You for hearing my prayers and loving me unconditionally. Please give me the strength, wisdom, and determination to walk in the center of Your will. In Jesus' name, Amen.*

If you've just received Jesus as your Lord and Savior, you've just made the very best decision you will ever make! There is absolutely nothing more important in this life or the next than having a personal relationship with God.

Of course, this does not mean you will never sin again. Rather, it signifies that the Lord will not count your transgressions against you in an eternal sense because Jesus Himself guarantees your redemption (Eph. 1:13–14). There may be consequences for your sins—for example, if you steal, you may have to make restitution, etc. Likewise, you may feel shame or pride because of your choices, which then keeps you from choosing fellowship with the Father even though He promises: "If we confess our sins, He is faithful and righteous to forgive us our sins and to cleanse us from all unrighteousness" (1 John 1:9). But your mistakes will no longer separate you in any permanent manner from God's presence or love (Rom. 8:38–39).

Sadly, a misunderstanding of this is what causes many people to fear when it comes to having a relationship with the Father or thinking about meeting Him face-to-face. We worry that we don't measure up, that we haven't been "good enough," that we should have done more, or that we do not deserve His mercy. These are the same reasons anxieties arise as we wait for Him, aren't they?

But please allow me to put your fears to rest. As I said previously, *there is absolutely nothing you can do to earn His approval*. Ephesians 2:8–9 explains, "By grace you have been saved through faith; and that not of yourselves, it is the gift of God; not as a result of works, so that no one may boast."

This is a crucial part of knowing Him, friend—you must accept what He has done for you and why He has done it. The Lord *chose* to provide a way for you to be saved because of His amazing love for you (John 3:16). The Savior invites you to have a relationship with Him because of His wonderful, holy, caring character (John 10:11, 18). Remember, "God demonstrates His own love toward us, in that while we were yet sinners, Christ died for us" (Rom. 5:8). It was *His* sacrifice, not yours, that made you right with Him.

> A crucial part of knowing God is accepting what He has done for you and why He has done it.

Our motive for serving the Father is not to earn salvation. Rather, we serve God out of respect, gratefulness, and love for the One who has chosen to make you and me His own. He deserves our reverence, dedication, and loyalty. Why? Because of who He is and the eternity-transforming gift He has given us.

Therefore, if you are a believer and have experienced anxiety thinking about your last moments on earth, it may be because you have an erroneous or incomplete view of the Lord. And right now, I challenge you to put those fears to death once and for all by surrendering your life—and your understanding of who He is—to Him. He is faithful and trustworthy to teach you.

HE IS GOD

This brings us to our next point: *You must fully accept that He is GOD.* Don't just read past that, but think about it. Allow this truth to pierce your inner person. It is not enough to believe in Him or say He is God. Rather, in Psalm 46:10, He commands, "Be still, and *know* that I am God!" (NLT, emphasis added). Fully embrace the fact that He is the infinite, inscrutable, invincible, and incontrovertible Supreme Lord of all lords, who has utter power over every aspect of our universe and beyond. Be aware of His constant, loving presence with you. And then live in the light of that truth.

He is GOD. He is the Sovereign Creator—ruling over and in complete control of everything in existence. Consider all that this means. In Genesis 8:22, He promises, "While the earth remains, seedtime and harvest, and cold and heat, and summer and winter, and day and night shall not cease." Is there anyone on earth or in heaven who can stop the seasons from passing? Absolutely not. Can we change the Earth's rotation or keep it from completing its orbit around the sun? Of course we can't.

But God can. In fact, Joshua 10:13 tells us He did. When the Israelites were in need of sunlight to defeat their enemies the Amorites, Joshua prayed and the Lord answered him powerfully. "The sun stopped in the middle of the sky and did not hasten to go down for about a whole day." In other words, just like that, God stopped the Earth on its axis to give His people success. That wasn't a problem for Him. Likewise, scientists have not figured out how to create instruments that can get even within a million miles of the sun because of its intense heat and radiation.[4] But the Lord can hold it in His hand and command its path as He wishes (Gen. 1:14–17).

He is GOD. He is the limitless, unwavering, and undeniable living King of all kings throughout eternity. All the empires and governments in the world since time began—with all of their armies, weapons, military strategies, and technology—cannot even touch the Lord. Isaiah 40:15 (NLT) proclaims, "All the nations of the world are but a drop in the bucket. They are nothing more than dust on the scales. He picks up the whole earth as though it were a grain of sand."

How heavy is a speck of dust on a scale? It does not move it in the least. Likewise, the nations cannot affect God at all—regardless of how they may attempt to reject Him (Ps. 2:2–4). Rather, "It is He who changes the times and the epochs; He removes kings and establishes kings" (Dan. 2:21). He can annihilate them all with one thought—but doesn't because of His great mercy and desire for all people to come to salvation (2 Pet. 3:9).

He is GOD. He existed before time itself and is completely outside its hold. He tells us in Isaiah 46:9–10, "I am God, and there is no one like Me, *declaring the end from the beginning*, and from ancient times things which have not been done, saying, 'My purpose will be established, and I will accomplish all My good pleasure' " (emphasis added). You and I view time as linear. When we hear His promises, we think, *That is in the future.* But the Father has already seen the end and is reporting the reality to us—He has achieved all that He said He would do (Isa. 55:10–11). Time just has to catch up.

> The Father has already seen the end and is reporting the reality to us—He has achieved all that He said He would do.

He is GOD. And friend, He loves you! He will always do exactly as He says and will faithfully fulfill His promises. You can be absolutely certain that He will always act on your behalf in the very best way possible. In fact, He assures you, " 'I know the plans that I have for you,' declares the LORD, 'plans for welfare and not for calamity to give you a future and a hope. Then you will call upon Me and come and pray to Me, and I will listen to you. You will seek Me and find Me when you search for Me with all your heart' " (Jer. 29:11–13).

Your loving Lord is good and kind to you, and He is committed to seeing you through every trial you face. You can count on Him. You can rest in His faithfulness. Therefore, it is extremely crucial that when the Father has you wait, that you *direct* your focus to Him by recalling His awesome power and attributes.

HE IS OMNISCIENT

The first important characteristic of God you should recall in times of waiting is that *He is omniscient*—He is all-knowing and unfathomably wise (Isa. 55:8–9). He is intimately aware of everything in your past, present, and future and every detail about your personality, giftedness, wants, dreams, desires, weaknesses, and frailties. There is nothing about you that ever catches Him by surprise.

Likewise, the Lord knows exactly what is going on in every situation that concerns you—even circumstances far into the future that you could not imagine. This is why He promises, "I will instruct you and teach you in the way which you should go; I will counsel you with My eye upon you" (Ps. 32:8). Knowing so much about you, the Father lovingly trains and prepares you for what is ahead—refining your faith and teaching you lessons that will eventually lead to your success. He directs you wisely—helping you avoid pitfalls and embrace opportunities that are important for your future.

One man who came to understand this well was Mordecai, the cousin of Queen Esther. He lived in the fifth century BC, during the time of the Persian Empire, in the city of Susa. Though many of the Jewish people had traveled back to their homeland in Jerusalem after the Babylonian captivity ended, most remained in the homes and businesses they'd built over the years. Such was the case for Mordecai. We are told:

While Mordecai was sitting at the king's gate, Bigthan and Teresh, two of the king's officials from those who guarded the door, became angry and sought to lay hands on King Ahasuerus. But the plot became known to Mordecai and he told Queen Esther, and Esther informed the king in Mordecai's name. Now when the plot was investigated and found to be so, they were both hanged on a gallows; and it was written in the Book of the Chronicles in the king's presence. (Esth. 2:21–23)

What Mordecai did saved King Ahasuerus's life. Of course, both the custom and the Persian law dictated that the monarch celebrate such heroic acts. Inexplicably, the days and months passed and Mordecai's bravery went unacknowledged. One can imagine that such an oversight was extremely disheartening to this good man.

Sadly, not only was Mordecai not honored, but over the next five years his situation deteriorated as well. A wicked man named Haman rose to power in the Persian government. Though King Ahasuerus commanded everyone to pay Haman respect, Mordecai refused to kneel before him (Esth. 3:2). Why? Because Haman was an Agagite—a descendent of the evil Amalekites, who were sworn enemies of Israel. The rivalry between them had raged for centuries—beginning as the Israelites made their escape from Egypt. Exodus 17:14–16 tells us, "The LORD said to Moses, 'Write this in a book as a memorial and recite it to Joshua, that I will utterly blot out the memory of Amalek from under heaven.' Moses built an altar and named it The LORD is My Banner; and he said, 'The LORD has sworn; the LORD will have war against Amalek from generation to generation.' " So Mordecai could not possibly pay homage to the enemy of God.

However, as often happens, standing for the Lord has ramifications. Esther 3:5–6 (NLT) reports, "When Haman saw that Mordecai would not bow down or show him respect, he was filled with rage. He had learned of Mordecai's nationality, so he decided it was not enough to lay hands on Mordecai alone. Instead, he looked for a way to destroy all the Jews throughout the entire empire." This evil man eagerly planned the mass genocide of the Jewish people and built gallows on which to hang Mordecai. It seemed Mordecai's circumstances could not get any worse. Perhaps he wondered—as many of us would—if God had forgotten him. His time appeared to be running out.

In fact, it was the very night before Haman planned to ask the king if he could have Mordecai executed when Ahasuerus felt an unusual restlessness and found he could not sleep. Perhaps you recall this story. Esther 6:1–3 recounts, "He gave an order to bring the book of records, the chronicles, and they were read before the king. It was found written what Mordecai had reported concerning Bigthana and Teresh, two of the king's eunuchs who were doorkeepers, that they had sought to lay hands on King Ahasuerus. The king said, 'What honor or dignity has been bestowed on Mordecai for this?' " What a moment for the king to realize his neglected duty and recall Mordecai's bravery!

Although it was a long wait, there was no more perfect moment for Mordecai to receive his reward.

Yet this is the perfect illustration of how the Father's omniscience and perfect timing work on our behalf. God—in His perfect knowledge and wisdom—knew in advance that Mordecai would need to come to King Ahasuerus's attention at just the right instant. And so five years prior, He set everything in motion to save Mordecai and the lives of all the Jewish people still residing in the provinces of Persia. Although it was a long wait, I'm absolutely certain there was no more perfect moment for Mordecai to receive his reward.

So as you consider the delays you are experiencing, understand that God has not forgotten you. On the contrary, He has allowed this season for a purpose because there are issues He knows about that you cannot yet see. But you are promised that if you will respect His leadership, He will teach you the path to choose (Ps. 25:12). Do not lose heart. Focus on Him and trust Him to provide in His perfect wisdom and time.

And when thoughts of despair arise because that blessing you're waiting for continues to delay, turn your thoughts to Him in prayer:

Lord, You know. You see my heart and understand the pain and anxiety that this time of waiting is causing me. But Father, I also realize that You are having me wait because of Your perfect wisdom and knowledge of the situation. And so I thank You, Father, that though I cannot see the purpose for the delay, I can know for certain it is for my ultimate benefit and blessing. I praise Your holy name for Your wonderful timing, attention to detail, and protection.

Father, You promise in James that if I lack wisdom, I can ask You for it and You will give it generously and without reproach (1:5). So Lord, in faith, I ask for Your understanding and perspective of my circumstances. I want to learn what You are teaching me.

Thank You for giving me the mind of Christ and drawing me closer to You in this situation. And thank You that in Your perfect, unfailing wisdom, You are arranging all details for my good and Your glory. In Jesus' name I pray, Amen.

HE IS OMNIPRESENT

While you are waiting, the second attribute to recall is that God is *omnipresent*, which means, *He is everywhere.* This is comforting because you can know for certain that you are always within God's reach—you can never be separated from His love no matter where you are or who threatens you (Rom. 8:38–39).

However, it is even more accurate to say that *everything is in the Lord's presence.* He is greater than the totality of creation. Nothing exists outside of Him. From the highest peaks of the Earth on Mount Everest in the Himalayas or Mount Chimborazo in Ecuador, to the lowest point of the ocean in the Marianas Trench and the deepest crevices of the Earth's core, the Father is there. Every planet, star, and solar system is well within His care. Even the farthest galaxies we've been able to detect with the Hubble Space Telescope—which, according to astronomers are more than thirteen billion light-years from Earth—are easily encompassed within His presence.

What does this mean for you? It signifies that the Lord is where you cannot be—accomplishing what concerns you. For example, we read in 2 Kings 6 that the ruler of Aram plotted to attack and destroy Israel. "He counseled with his servants saying, 'In such and such a place shall be my camp' " (v. 8). Now, there was no spy there to hear his plans and no traitor among his counselors to inform Israel of the attack that was coming. But God was there. He notified His prophet Elisha of their location and effectively safeguarded the Israelites from the Arameans (vv. 9–12).

Likewise, you never know where the Father is working on Your behalf—turning circumstances to your favor or inspiring others to speak out for your benefit.

For Mordecai, it was the chronicler who recorded his brave deeds and King Ahasuerus who eventually saved his life. Mordecai could not have appeared before the monarch on his own accord—but God was well able to reach him.

> You never know where the Father is working on Your behalf—turning circumstances to your favor or inspiring others to speak out for your benefit.

For the Lahu people, it was William Marcus Young who traveled from the United States to Kengtung, Burma, to share the gospel with them. They had no way to travel so far to find a willing missionary. But "the eyes of the LORD move to and fro throughout the earth that He may strongly support those whose heart is completely His" (2 Chron. 16:9). The Father knew exactly who to call to reach them.

The same is true for you. Even now, you may have no earthly idea where the Lord is raising up an answer to your prayers—but He is. Even better, your immense, awesome, majestic God has chosen to make His dwelling place in your heart. Walking with you always. Going before you to prepare the way. Carrying you in times of trouble. Following behind you, ensuring that all you do in obedience to Him has lasting fruit. And He is so intimately in tune with every sub-atomic particle of your body and aspect of your inner person—your desires, painful wounds, hurtful memories, and hopeful dreams—that He is providing for your needs even before you can know you have them.

So when thoughts about the blessing you're waiting for begin to dishearten you, turn your heart to Him in prayer:

> *Father, how grateful I am that not only are You here with me right now, but You are working in places and people that I cannot even imagine— engineering circumstances for my good. I cannot begin to guess all the ways You have protected me from unseen dangers, orchestrated situations for my edification, and arranged blessings from unexpected sources. I have absolutely no reason to fear. At times I feel as if my sphere of influence is so small, but I am so very thankful that because You are omnipresent, Your ability to govern situations is completely unhindered.*
>
> *Father, I pray that as Your eyes move to and fro throughout the earth, that You will find my heart to be completely dedicated to You. So Lord, search me, examine my thoughts, and cast out any hurtful way in me, so that I may please You in every way. Lead me in doing Your will, Father. And thank You for being my ever-present help in every circumstance. In Jesus' name I pray, Amen.*

HE IS OMNIPOTENT

Third, during seasons of waiting, it is crucial for you to remember that *God is absolutely omnipotent*—all-powerful and greater in strength than every other force combined. He can do anything He chooses to do at anytime because the Lord is the supreme authority over all that exists. And because He is all-powerful, even the obstacles and trials in your life that seem to impede or thwart God's plan are actually tools He uses to fulfill His purposes when you keep your focus on Him.

First Provision: God gives the promised land to Abraham.
Think about the Lord's promise to Abraham concerning the territory
we know as Israel. This small but crucial area forms an important cross-
roads between Europe, Asia, and Africa, and has long been fought over
because of its immensely strategic location. Understanding the region's
tremendous significance, the Father told Abraham, "To your descendants *I will* give this land" (Gen. 12:7, emphasis added).

Don't miss the pivotal words in the covenant between the Lord
and Abraham: *I will.* This was not a conditional agreement God was
offering; it was not contingent upon anything Abraham could do. Yes,
Abraham was to walk before Him obediently, but the Lord was clear—
it was up to Him to give Abraham the land of Canaan. From the very
beginning, God took *full responsibility* for fulfilling His promise. And
He did. Genesis 13:14–18 records that the Lord provided Abraham with
the gift He'd promised him.

*Second Provision: God restores the land to Abraham's descendants after
freeing them from exile in Egypt.*
But as you may recall, Abraham's descendants—Jacob, his twelve
sons, and their families—lived there until a severe famine drove them
to Egypt for food. They moved to the province of Goshen (Gen. 46)
and ended up staying in that lush, fruitful land for four hundred
years. Unfortunately, there arose a pharaoh who enslaved the Israelites
and treated them cruelly. So they cried out to the Lord for His help.
Exodus 2:24 tells us, "God heard their groaning; and God remem-
bered His covenant with Abraham, Isaac, and Jacob." The time had
come for Him to bring them back into the land He had promised
Abraham.

Freedom from pharaoh seemed impossible, of course. How would
they escape his grasp? They were slaves. They had no army, weapons, or
strength. But more important, no other people had ever successfully re-
captured their territories after so many afflictions and such a long time

away—especially a nation as militarily weak as Israel was at that point. During Israel's four hundred years away from Canaan, other nations—specifically the Amorites, Hittites, Perizzites, Girgashites, Canaanites, Hivites, and Jebusites—had inhabited the land and set up reinforcements. They were not going to be easy to oust.

But as we know, Almighty God honored His promise. He raised up Moses to lead them back to the Promised Land. And Scripture reports, "The Lord gave Israel all the land which He had sworn to give to their fathers, and they possessed it and lived in it . . . Not one of the good promises which the Lord had made to the house of Israel failed; all came to pass" (Josh. 21:43, 45).

Was it the Israelites who accomplished this? No. It was their awesome, omnipotent God. And Moses praised Him, saying, "*The Lord* heard our voice and saw our affliction and our toil and our oppression; and *the Lord* brought us out of Egypt with a mighty hand and an outstretched arm and with great terror and with signs and wonders; and *He has brought us* to this place and has given us this land, a land flowing with milk and honey" (Deut. 26:7–9, emphasis added).

> Was it the Israelites who accomplished this? No. It was their awesome, omnipotent God.

Third Provision: God returns Abraham's descendants to the promised land after delivering them from the Babylonian captivity.

Several hundred years later, a similar situation arose. Because of her sinful practices and disobedience, Israel was invaded by Assyria in 722 BC, and her people were scattered among the empire's provinces (2 Kings 17:22–24). Likewise, Israel's sister nation to the south, Judah, was invaded and eventually overcome by the Babylonians (605–586 BC), and her people were deported far from their homeland (2 Chron. 36:14–20).

Again it seemed as if the Jewish people would never return to the land of their inheritance. Although they had been miraculously restored to the Promised Land after their bondage in Egypt, it seemed unfeasible that it could happen a second time. But the exiles held on to the hope that their omnipotent God would return them to their beloved homeland.

And true to God's word, the situation changed radically in 539 BC when the Persian king Cyrus conquered the Babylonians. As prophesied more than one hundred years earlier by Isaiah (44:28; 45:1–6) and also by Jeremiah (25:12; 29:10), Cyrus declared, "The LORD, the God of heaven, has given me all the kingdoms of the earth, and He has appointed me to build Him a house in Jerusalem, which is in Judah. Whoever there is among you of all His people, may the LORD his God be with him, and let him go up!" (2 Chron. 36:23). God Himself changed King Cyrus's heart. So, again, the Jewish people were permitted to return to their land. For the third time, He gave them the territories He'd promised Abraham.

How right and true the prophet Jeremiah's words, "LORD God! Behold, You have made the heavens and the earth by Your great power and by Your outstretched arm! Nothing is too difficult for You" (Jer. 32:17).

Fourth Provision: God re-establishes Abraham's descendants as a nation in the promised land after nineteen centuries.
Now, some may believe it would have been enough for God to give Israel its land three times. If the people lost the territory because of sinfulness or other tactical errors, why should the Lord have to restore it to them again and again? Yet that is how seriously the Father views His promises—He would not change His opinion or fail His servant Abraham. Yes, there would be consequences when the people disobeyed the Lord, but ultimately, His word would stand (Neh. 9:31).

Of course, there was no time in history when this was more difficult to believe than the last time the children of Israel were exiled from the land. In AD 66, the Jewish people attempted the Great Revolt against the oppression and persecution of the Roman government, which had ruled

them since 63 BC. This turned out to be a disastrous decision, resulting
in the destruction of Jerusalem and the Temple in AD 70. It was the first
of three wars between the Jewish people and the Romans, which would
ultimately result in the expulsion of Abraham's descendants from the
area.

AD 66–73	The First Jewish–Roman War: The Great Revolt
AD 70	Fall of Jerusalem and Destruction of the Temple
AD 115–117	The Second Jewish–Roman War: The Kitos War
AD 132–136	The Third Jewish–Roman War: The Bar Kokhba Revolt
AD 138	The Jewish people are banned from entering Jerusalem except on Tisha B'Av
AD 1882	Aliyahs begin
AD 1917	Balfour Declaration
AD 1922	British Mandate for Palestine
May 14, 1948	Establishment of the State of Israel

Centuries passed. Though the Jewish people repeatedly tried to
recapture their land by many means, they experienced setback after
setback—never fully able to re-establish their hold over the territory.
Only a very small remnant was able to endure there.

Many probably wondered where God was. Hadn't He promised
Abraham the land would belong to his descendants? Had the Lord not
told them, "I will take you from the nations, gather you from all the
lands and bring you into your own land" through the prophet Ezekiel
(36:24)? Had He rejected them forever?

The situation became even worse at the end of the 1800s. Though the
Jewish people had always experienced persecution, it intensified with a
series of *pogroms*—or violent attacks, riots, and organized massacres—
throughout Russia, Yemen, Romania, Poland, Germany, and other nations. This resulted in five *aliyahs*—or waves of immigration—by Jews
to Palestine for safety. But even there they did not find much peace. The

Ottoman Empire, which controlled the territory, was openly hostile to its Jewish residents.

Again, God raised up leaders who understood the need to restore the Jewish people to their homeland. After World War I, with the fall of the Ottoman Empire in Palestine, the League of Nations passed the British Mandate, which recognized the United Kingdom's rule over the area known today as the State of Israel, the West Bank, and the Gaza Strip. The British had stated that they were favorable to the formation of a national home for the Jewish people in the Balfour Declaration of 1917—so descendants of Abraham throughout the world began to see a very real possibility that God would restore the land of their inheritance, despite Arab resistance.

> Yes, it had taken a long time, but God had not failed them. The land belonged to Israel.

Then after World War II, because of the atrocities committed against the Jewish people in the Holocaust and the tumultuous situation in the territory, the British government did something only God could have engineered—it resolved to pull out of Palestine and proposed a partition plan. This momentous decision eventually paved the way for the establishment of the State of Israel on May 14, 1948. The Lord God Almighty had done it again—He had fulfilled His promise. Seemingly impossible prophecy had come to pass. Yes, it had taken a long time, but God had not failed them. The land belonged to Israel.

Of course, this is obviously a very simplified version of Israel's long and complicated history, and all of us are well aware of how the Israelis still suffer today. The point here is not to dissect the past, but to show the power and faithfulness of Almighty God—directing nations; turning the hearts of leaders to His purposes; and returning His scattered, persecuted people to that crucial territory—not once, but *three* times.

No other nation in history has ever come back into existence after disappearing from the world stage for nineteen terrible, affliction-filled centuries—but Israel did. No matter how horrific the persecution or how intensely the wicked tried to exterminate them, Abraham's descendants maintained their identity, survived, and have come back stronger and more fruitful than ever. They returned to a desert wasteland and have transformed Israel into a beautiful, fruitful place that is a marvel of modern technology—exactly as was foretold in prophecy (Ezek. 36:29–30, 34–36).

And as I sit here and consider the Lord's favor on Israel, I can only think of how absolutely foolish it is for any country or group that attempts to take the land from the Jewish people. Enemies of this favored nation are not fighting against mere flesh and bone—they are opposing almighty, omnipotent, all-powerful God who made the promise!

Friend, the Lord loves Israel. The Father is still actively keeping His covenant with His people today because He cares about them. It was in deep grief that our Savior cried out, "Jerusalem, Jerusalem, who kills the prophets and stones those who are sent to her! How often I wanted to gather your children together, the way a hen gathers her chicks under her wings" (Matt. 23:37). How desperately He wants them to come to knowledge of the truth and be saved. And so today He is drawing Jews throughout the world back to Himself—showing them that He, Jesus, is indeed the promised Messiah they've been looking for.

So, as Scripture instructs, I "pray for the peace of Jerusalem" (Ps. 122:6) and for the salvation of the Jewish people—because that is what is important to our Savior's heart. I hope you will too. May they realize their Messiah has come and that He loves them dearly.

But perhaps you are wondering, *What does all this have to do with me?* Simply this: The Jewish people are Abraham's *physical* children, but as a believer in Jesus Christ, you are Abraham's *spiritual* offspring. As we are told in Galatians 3:6–7, "Abraham believed God, and it was reckoned to him as righteousness. Therefore, be sure that it is those who are of faith who are sons of Abraham."

If the Lord has done so much for the people Israel—who have not yet accepted Christ—how much more would He do for a person who eagerly loves and serves Jesus?

Friend, take this to heart. The Father can accomplish *anything* He's promised you—even what looks absolutely, unalterably impossible. You can always trust Him to keep His word to you regardless of how challenging your circumstances may appear. Why? Because "the LORD has established His throne in the heavens, and His sovereignty rules over all" (Ps. 103:19). Not only is He *able* to help you, He has the *authority* and *desire* to do so.

> The Father can accomplish *anything* He's promised you— even what looks absolutely, unalterably impossible.

So do not be afraid (Isa. 41:9–10). Rather, have faith that He is turning circumstances to your favor. Because, as I said before, there is one thing that is absolutely sure—you will never go wrong trusting in the all-powerful, omnipotent God who defends, directs, provides for, and protects you.

So as with the other attributes, when the time of waiting grows long and you grow discouraged, turn your thoughts to your almighty heavenly Father in prayer:

Father, how grateful I am that You are my God—my omnipotent King of kings and sovereign Ruler of all creation. Lord, my problems seem so overwhelming because of my limitations, but I know they are nothing for You. You are God! You are the One who arranged the sun, moon, and stars in the heavens; gave Israel to the descendants of Abraham four times; and who knows my life from beginning to end. With the prophet Jeremiah, I say, "Nothing is too difficult for You!"

I thank You, Father, for remembering that I am dust—weak and inadequate in so many ways. Ultimately, this is what causes me fear, dear Lord. I cannot accomplish what I need to on my own. This desire in my heart requires Your supernatural intervention. Without You, I am without hope. But Lord God, even in this, I thank and praise You because I know this need has come about in my life so You can reveal Your mighty power, protection, and provision to me. I know that none of this is by mistake, but is the perfect platform for demonstrating Your glory.

So I focus not on my weakness, Father, but on Your awesome strength. This battle is not mine to overcome, but Yours to win. I cannot, but You can! When I am weak—You are mighty! So thank You for loving and providing for me. To You be all honor, glory, power, and praise now and forever. In Jesus' name I pray, Amen.

HE IS LOVING

Of course, God's wisdom, presence, and power have even more profound significance because of His fourth attribute—*His perfect, unconditional love for you.* Not only *can* He help you, but because of His profound, everlasting, impassioned commitment to you, you can be certain *He will.* The Father's unfailing care means you can be absolutely certain that He will employ all of His supernatural attributes and resources for your ultimate benefit. But you can also know that this time of waiting is for an extremely good reason (Rom. 8:28).

Friend, people may have let you down in the past, which makes you hesitant to trust others. But understand that God's love for you is not like most human love—moody, unpredictable, self-serving, and contingent upon your response. His tenderness toward you is based on His holy character—which is unwavering, sacrificial, unchanging, completely trustworthy, and committed to providing the very best for you.

In fact, 1 John 4:8 explains that love is His very nature: "God is love." In other words, He cannot cease to care for you, because in order to do so He would have to stop being Himself. Likewise, your heavenly Father won't love you more when you're obedient or less when you're sinful, because His affection is based on His unchanging disposition—not on your worthiness.

This is why you can count on God to help you as you wait on Him. He is loving and faithful. You never have to worry about Him saying one thing and doing another or acting in a harmful way toward you.

Instead, you can count on the wonderful assurances He gives you every day of your life. He gives us ten powerful assurances:

1. *His lovingkindness and compassion are yours every day.* Lamentations 3:22–23 says, "The Lord's lovingkindnesses indeed never cease, for His compassions never fail. They are new every morning; great is Your faithfulness." You can always rely on the Father's faithful love for you—to guide you throughout your day, comfort you in difficulty, and lead you into the future. No matter how you failed yesterday or what burden you have to carry, His love for you today is fresh, new, and steadfastly unwavering. He will never leave you or forsake you (Deut. 31:8). And you can know for certain that He is working on your behalf every day of your life.

2. *He is a solid, unshakable foundation for you.* Jesus said, "Everyone who hears these words of Mine and acts on them, may be compared to a wise man who built his house on the rock. And the rain fell, and the floods came, and the winds blew and slammed against that house; and yet it did not fall, for it had been founded on the rock." God is unchanging, and His Word is trustworthy. If the Lord were given to sudden and volatile alterations in His behavior or commands, He would be unreliable. But our loving, heavenly Father is dependable and stable, and He operates on fixed, timeless principles that you and I can count upon to lead us to success (Heb. 13:8). This is why we can build our lives on His promises and trust Him in the delays. He has been unwaveringly faithful in the past, and He will continue to be so in the future (Heb. 10:23). And you can be certain that no matter what comes, if you focus on Him, He will hold you steady and secure.

3. *He will guide you in the way you should go.* Proverbs 3:5–6 promises, "Trust in the Lord with all your heart and do not

lean on your own understanding. In all your ways acknowledge Him, and He will make your paths straight." You don't
have to know the best path for your life or toward what you
are waiting for—God is faithful to lead you. He understands
the safest, most effective, most efficient way to take you—the
road that prepares you perfectly for what is ahead. Though it
may not be the route you would have
chosen for yourself—and it may be
taking longer than you'd like—you can
be assured that as long as you keep your
eyes on Him, you are right on track.

Our loving,
heavenly Father
is dependable and
stable, and He
operates on fixed,
timeless principles
that you and I can
count upon to lead
us to success.

4. *Whatever He requires of you, He will
enable you to accomplish.* First Thessalonians 5:24 promises, "Faithful is He
who calls you, and He also will bring it
to pass." This is especially important to
remember as you are waiting on God.
Many times, as He delays, you may be tempted to worry
because it appears your resources are diminishing far past
where you are comfortable. But this is for the very purpose
of exercising your faith in Him. The Lord God has a supernatural way of multiplying your time, talents, strength,
wisdom, and supply when you trust Him (Judg. 6).

5. *He will discipline you when needed for your own good.*
Psalm 119:75 tells us, "I know, O LORD, that Your judgments
are righteous, and that *in faithfulness* You have afflicted me"
(emphasis added). In other words, like the good Father that
He is, He corrects you to remove whatever in your life is
holding you back, causing you pain, making you stumble,
or doesn't fit you as His child. For example, say there was a
dream job you really wanted. If there were some aspect of
your personality or how you respond to others that would
completely undermine your effectiveness and ability to

succeed at that occupation, wouldn't you want the Lord to remove it? Remember, the Father sees all your blind spots, wounds, and places of spiritual bondage that you cannot perceive. So out of love for you, He disciplines you—freeing you from what would ultimately destroy you and helping you become all you were created to be (Heb. 12:5–11).

6. *He will limit the pressure of your trials and temptations to what you can bear.* In 1 Corinthians 10:13, He assures you, "No temptation has overtaken you but such as is common to man; and God is faithful, who will not allow you to be tempted beyond what you are able, but with the temptation will provide the way of escape also, so that you will be able to endure it." Because of His great love, the Father protects you from enduring too much hardship or pressure—which thankfully means there is also a limit to the time you will have to wait. Of course, it may not always seem that way, and you may wonder why He would allow you to suffer in the first place. But realize that He knows your great potential—what you can achieve and overcome—if you will learn to trust Him. And there is nothing that will stretch you, refine your character, and strengthen your faith in Him like adversity (Rom. 5:3–5).

7. *He will forgive your sins.* The Lord guarantees in 1 John 1:9, "If we confess our sins, He is faithful and righteous to forgive us our sins and to cleanse us from all unrighteousness." This means two very important facts. First, once you confess your sin, the Father no longer holds it against you. Therefore, you have no reason to fear that He isn't blessing you because of some mistake in the past. Psalm 103:12 testifies, "As far as the east is from the west, so far has He removed our transgressions from us." But second, it means the Lord will reveal what is causing you to sin if you will listen to Him. Remember, your transgressions begin with your

thoughts—some way you want to meet your needs on your own apart from God. The Father will not only guide you in identifying those thoughts, but He'll help you overcome them (2 Cor. 10:5).

8. *He will always keep His promises to you.* Scripture proclaims, "Not one word has failed of all His good promise" (1 Kings 8:56). When it comes to your loving, heavenly Father, there should be absolutely no question in your mind about whether or not He will do as He says. He is holy, honorable, and truthful—He would never lie to you (Titus 1:2). You can count on the fact that He will do exactly as He says—just as He has all throughout history. Though the promise may take a different form than you anticipated, may take longer to arrive than you expected, and may appear in a way you never imagined, God will keep His word. So be assured—the Father will not fail you.

9. *He will keep you eternally secure.* Jesus affirmed, "I give eternal life to them, and they will never perish; and no one will snatch them out of My hand" (John 10:28). As I said earlier in this chapter, the great blessing of your salvation is that it is based entirely upon the love and provision of Christ. There is nothing you can do to earn it; therefore, there is nothing you can do to lose it. Accept that it is yours by faith.

10. *He has prepared an eternal home in heaven for you.* Finally, in John 14:2–3, Jesus promises, "In My Father's house are many dwelling places; if it were not so, I would have told you; for I go to prepare a place for you. If I go and prepare a place for you, I will come again and receive you to Myself, that where I am, there you may be also." Heaven will be the most joyful, peaceful, fulfilling home you can possibly imagine—one that can never be marred or taken away. You will finally be in the presence of the One who died for you—without anything hindering your fellowship with Him. Your faith will

become sight and He will reward all you did in obedience
to Him.

Friend, do you really believe that the God who loves you so much
would give you less than what is actually best for you? Of course He
wouldn't! Now, you may ask for something that—for reasons known
only to Him—is less than ideal for you. So He may say, "No" or "Wait"
because He wants you to have a blessing that is far better. But in every
situation, you can rely upon Him, claiming the promise of Romans 8:32,
"He who did not spare His own Son, but delivered Him over for us all,
how will He not also with Him freely give us all things?"

So when you are fearful and doubtful because the delays seem to last
too long, turn your thoughts to your loving Savior in prayer:

*My loving, heavenly Father, I know that You are good, kind, and compas-
sionate. Thank You for caring for me, being my secure foundation, leading
me in the way I should go, teaching me Your ways, limiting my suffering,
forgiving my sins, freeing me from bondage, and giving me an eternal home
in heaven with You. Truly, in Your grace, You have given me far better than
I deserve. Thank You for blessing me and making me completely worthy
through Jesus.*

*Father, knowing that You have permitted this time of waiting because of
Your great love for me helps me to bear it. Thank You for not allowing me
to settle for mediocre blessings—but always giving me Your very best.*

*Father, teach me what You would have me learn and increase my love
for You daily. And thank You, my Lord and my God, that neither death
nor life, angels nor demons, not my fears for today nor my worries about
tomorrow, nothing I can do or have failed to do, no power in the sky above
or on earth or in all creation—not even all of the forces of the enemy—can
separate me from Your love that You've given me through my wonderful
Savior Jesus. I praise You, Father. In Jesus' name I pray, Amen.*

DIRECT YOUR FOCUS

Who better to focus on than the almighty, all-powerful, all-knowing, and unconditionally loving God? He is unquestionably trustworthy in every moment, situation, and circumstance no matter what. He is God—your wise Counselor, omnipresent Provider, omnipotent Defender, and loving Father. He is the One you are waiting for. He knows what is absolutely best for you, and He can and will accomplish it for you. You also know that if He does not give you what you want, it is undoubtedly for your protection. Why then would you be afraid?

Of course, directing your focus to God is often easier said than done. This is because there are often strongholds in your heart that prevent you from completely trusting the Father. And so, you must not only allow Him to remove that bondage, but also let Him teach you the discipline of keeping your mind on Him. We will discuss this more in the next chapter.

> You never gain by getting ahead of the Lord, and you never lose by waiting upon Him.

The most important thing, however, is for you to keep in mind that you never gain by getting ahead of the Lord, and you never lose by waiting upon Him. Therefore, live in the awareness of His presence. Direct your focus to Him and expect Him to reveal His awesome plan for your life to you. And be confident because, "Indeed, none of those who wait for [God] will be ashamed" (Ps. 25:3).

Father, how grateful I am that I can wait upon You and know for certain I will not be put to shame. When my heart wavers, Lord, please remind me to direct my focus to You. You are omniscient—knowing and understanding what I cannot conceive. You are omnipresent—going where I cannot go and raising solutions I don't even realize exist. You are omnipotent—accomplishing all I am powerless to achieve. And You are loving—always providing what is most beneficial for me. Even when You direct me away from something I think I want desperately, I thank You, knowing You are protecting me and leading me to an ever greater blessing.

Lord, You are GOD! You are the sovereign, everlasting King of kings and Lord of lords. And You love me. I have absolutely no reason to fear no matter how many days or months or years go by. You will not fail or forsake me. And just as You formed the Earth, sun, moon, and stars—You will form a solution for the deepest yearnings of my heart. Thank You, Father. I can always count on You! In Your holy name I pray, dearest Jesus. Amen.

POINTS FOR ACTIVE WAITING

1. Memorize Psalm 62:5–6: "My soul, wait in silence for God only, for my hope is from Him. He only is my rock and my salvation, my stronghold; I shall not be shaken."
2. Whenever you feel anxious or sorrowful because of what you are waiting for, repeat Psalm 27:14 and Psalm 62:5–6 to yourself.
3. Review God's attributes. Ask Him to make His characteristics real to you and reveal how He is working in your situation. Write your discoveries in the space provided or in your journal and remind yourself about them as often as necessary.
4. As discussed in the beginning of this chapter, it is extremely important that you train your mind not to focus on what you lack or on your circumstances—but that you direct your thoughts to the Lord. So whenever you grow discouraged, remember to thank God for His attributes: His omniscience, omnipresence, omnipotence, and unconditional love that He employs to provide the very best for you. If you're not sure how to do so, use the prayers that are included throughout this chapter.

Use this space to respond to the "Points for Active Waiting" and to record prayer requests, key lessons God is teaching you, and your insights about waiting on the Lord to act on your behalf.

Trust in the LORD with all your heart
and do not lean on your own understanding.
In all your ways acknowledge Him,
and He will make your paths straight.
—Proverbs 3:5–6

SURRENDERING YOUR FOCUS

Identifying the Idols that Impede Your Faith

There is an inherent battle that occurs when we wait on God—perhaps you feel it today. As the weeks and months pass, we struggle with knowing His will and whether what we desire is different from what He has purposed. We know the Lord is omniscient, omnipresent, omnipotent, and loving, as we saw in the last chapter. We want to trust and honor Him. But we sense that there must be some intrinsic conflict between what we pray for and what the Father has planned for us because we do not see Him answering us. And all the while, the enemy is whispering in our ear, telling us how irrational it is to trust a God we do not see with issues that are so significant to us. We try to have faith, but it seems that no matter what we do, our hearts are bent toward despair.

Of course, as we've discussed previously, what we want and what the Father desires for us are not necessarily different. For example, we know that Abraham wanted a son and God promised to give him one. But we read verses like Psalm 37:4, "Delight yourself in the LORD; and He will give you the desires of your heart," and we wonder if we can truly trust Him with our most precious hopes. After all, He has not moved or carried through with His promise. He hasn't taken the desire away either—though we've begged Him to do so. Does this mean we should be doing something about it ourselves? Why is God delaying? Does He care? Should we even serve Him if He would deny us such important requests?

Eventually, a stressful tension arises between our inmost longings and our desire to honor the Father, and it is caused by *the emphasis we place on what we yearn for*. Remember what we discussed earlier: waiting signifies an expectant endurance that is demonstrated by a *directed*, *purposeful*, *active*, and *courageous* attitude of prayer. And the first characteristic of godly waiting is *directing our focus to God*. When we find it difficult to center our attention on the Father, it indicates that He is not our ultimate priority, as we may believe.

Now, this is not a conflict that only affects weak or new believers. This battle can occur in any one of us. In fact, we see it in Abraham's life, though he is one of the greatest examples of faith in Scripture (Rom. 4:3). But our problem is that we focus on our *questions* far more than on the Father's ability to *answer* them. And the more we think about the desire of our heart instead of God, the more frustrated we become and the more tempted we are to take matters into our own hands.

> We want what we want—even more, at times, than we want Him.

We may *want* to focus on the Father, and we may actively try to do so. After all, He is sovereign—He knows what is most beneficial for us and loves us so much He will not settle for less than His very best. Yet we are still in turmoil. We want what we want—even more, at times, than we want Him. We long to figure it all out, guess what He will do, and perhaps "help" Him accomplish what He has promised us. And this, my friends, can get us in all sorts of trouble.

GODLY MAN, INDICATIVE CHOICES

Of course, there are not many people who will have to wait as long as Abraham did to see their hearts' desires fulfilled. It was not until he was seventy-five that God promised Abraham to give him a fruitful land, many descendants, and make him into a prosperous nation—ensuring his legacy (Gen. 12:1–7). I imagine Abraham and his wife, Sarah, had wanted children from the time they were married—which meant they had longed to have a baby *for several decades*. But it was not until they are actually "past childbearing" age (Gen. 18:11) that God gave them this amazing promise, "I will make your descendants as the dust of the earth, so that if anyone can number the dust of the earth, then your descendants can also be numbered" (Gen. 13:16). No doubt they were anxious to see the Lord start with even one. Just like Abraham, we too sometimes try to get ahead of God, as we try to figure out His plan or somehow speed it along.

1. THE NEED TO FIGURE IT OUT

But Scripture reports that after some time passed, Abraham allowed the circumstances of his life to overcome his faith in God. In fact, he went as far as asking the Father, "O Lord GOD, what will You give me, since I am childless, and the heir of my house is Eliezer of Damascus? . . . You have given no offspring to me, one born in my house is my heir" (Gen. 15:2–3). Do you see what he was doing? There was no tangible evidence of God's working, so Abraham attempted to figure out what the Lord would do by his own logic.

We often do the same, don't we? When important puzzle pieces seem to be missing, we do not understand why the Father would allow them to remain hidden for so long. So we look around and search for earthly answers to our dilemma—blaming ourselves, others, our circumstances, bad influences, society, and even the Lord for the issues that confound us.

For Abraham, it was a big leap to imagine God would make him a great nation when he'd spent so many years trying to have offspring and still did not have even one child. In his mind, no baby meant the Lord could only work through his servant Eliezer to complete the promise. And trying to work out who was to be his successor—when it was not his right or responsibility to do so—led Abraham to doubt the living God and suffer terrible discouragement.

Of course, this is what usually happens when we try to use human logic to discern the divine plan. Whatever Abraham could imagine was far less wonderful than what the Father had actually arranged. Remember, God Himself tells us, "As the heavens are higher than the earth, so are My ways higher than your ways and My thoughts than your thoughts" (Isa. 55:9). He also promises that He "is able to do far more abundantly beyond all that we ask or think" (Eph. 3:20). In other words, we cannot possibly conceive of how the Lord is working everything out for us—and we will only frustrate ourselves if we try.

Thankfully, the Father clarified His intentions to Abraham, "This man will not be your heir; but one who will come forth from your own body, he shall be your heir" (Gen. 15:4). The Lord comforted and reassured Abraham, which is what He always does when we spend time in His presence. And Genesis 15:6 reports Abraham "believed in the LORD; and He reckoned it to him as righteousness."

Like Abraham, you do not need to understand all the details of God's plan for your life—nor can you. All you really need is to know what your next step of obedience should be. As Proverbs 3:5–6 instructs, "Trust in the LORD with all your heart and *do not lean on your own understanding.* In all your ways *acknowledge Him,* and *He will* make your paths straight" (emphasis added). If there are aspects of the Lord's calling or promises that do not make sense and seem to have missing puzzle pieces, that's all right. Your omniscient God knows what He is doing. So don't try to figure it all out. Just keep your eyes on the Father, and He will keep you on the right path.

2. THE TEMPTATION TO SPEED THE PLAN ALONG

Of course, we all know that time has a way on wearing on even the strongest faith—especially when the blessing is so important to us. As you and I can imagine, there had to be a great deal of fear, shame, embarrassment, cynicism, and pressure from others that Abraham and

Sarah had to combat every day in order to believe the Father would take care of them. Ten years had passed since God made His promise to Abraham and still there were no children. What was going on? And as often happens when we are waiting, the temptation to take matters into their own hands became great.

The couple must have examined the issue of their childlessness from every angle—focusing on the obstacles rather than on the Lord's ability to overcome them. Eventually, Sarah seemed to have surmised that she was the one hindering the fulfillment of God's purposes. So as many of us would do, Sarah came up with a plan—a bad one. She told Abraham, "Behold, the LORD has prevented me from bearing children. Please go in to my maid; perhaps I will obtain children through her" (Gen. 16:2). Rather than wait to see what the Lord would do, her idea was for Abraham to conceive a child with the Egyptian servant named Hagar—a practice that was common in their culture. Even worse, Abraham agreed to it.

We have all done it—we've all tried to "help" God and speed up His divine time line through our own means. And I have learned throughout my life that every time I get ahead of the Lord, I make a mess. Abraham certainly found that to be true as well.

> I have learned throughout my life that every time I get ahead of the Lord, I make a mess.

You probably know the story well. A baby named Ishmael was born from Abraham and Hagar's union, and a great deal of trouble ensued. First, there was terrible conflict between Sarah and Hagar—so much, in fact, that the Egyptian maid found it necessary to flee (Gen. 16:6). Second, the Lord made it very clear that this child, Ishmael, was not the promised successor, which must have broken Abraham's heart (Gen. 17:18–20). Third, when Isaac, the rightful heir, was born, there was enmity between Ishmael and Isaac, and Abraham was forced to drive Hagar and her son from the camp (Gen. 21:9–14).

The final consequence of Abraham and Sarah's actions, however, is most certainly the worst. The Lord said Ishmael would be "a wild donkey of a man, His hand will be against everyone, and everyone's hand will be against him; and he will live to the east of all his brothers" (Gen. 16:12). Likewise, Genesis 25:18 reports Ishmael's offspring "settled from Havilah to Shur which is east of Egypt as one goes toward Assyria; he settled in defiance of all his relatives." His descendants, the Ishmaelites, intermarried with the nations inhabiting this vast territory—from the Suez Canal through Sinai and north across the Saudi Peninsula to what is modern-day Iraq—and they became the Arab peoples who have been a constant source of conflict for Israel. In fact, the religion of Islam names Ishmael as one of its patriarchs and prophets—though it was not founded until much later in the seventh century AD.

But just think about how vastly different and undoubtedly more peaceful Israel's existence would be if Abraham and Sarah had simply waited on God and had not contrived their own way of making the promise come true. To this day their descendants are suffering the consequences of their actions.

Friend, do not make the same mistake. Don't get ahead of the Lord or try to wrestle control from His hands. Nothing good can ever come of it.

3. THE TEST TO PROVE WHAT REALLY RULES YOUR HEART

Now Abraham was eighty-six when Ishmael was born, and it was not until another thirteen years later—when he was ninety-nine—that God appeared to Abraham saying, "I will surely return to you at this time next year; and behold, Sarah your wife will have a son" (Gen. 18:10). So from the first time Abraham received the promise (at age seventy-five) to the fulfillment of it (at one hundred) was twenty-five years. That is a great deal of waiting. Perhaps, like me, you think, "Oh Lord, please don't make me wait so long!" But you can certainly imagine that after all that anticipation, his son, Isaac, was indeed very precious to him.

Nevertheless, after Abraham and Sarah had the boy and a few years passed, the Lord instructed Abraham to do something that completely shook his world. Genesis 22:1–2 reports, "It came about after these things, that God tested Abraham, and said to him, 'Abraham!' And he said, 'Here I am.' He said, 'Take now your son, your only son, whom you love, Isaac, and go to the land of Moriah, and offer him there as a burnt offering on one of the mountains of which I will tell you.' "

One can scarcely conceive of a more difficult command. But Scripture tells us the reason—the Lord was *testing* Abraham. The term used there for "tested" is the Hebrew word *nasah*, which means, "to try, assay, or prove," and this word is often used when referring to examining the quality of weapons. In other words, God was demonstrating the strength of Abraham's faith and what really ruled his heart. This was not for the Lord's benefit—He already knew all that was in Abraham. Rather, Abraham had to make the choice and recognize who truly came first in his life.

Thankfully, Genesis 22:3 testifies, "Abraham rose early in the morning and saddled his donkey, and took two of his young men with him and Isaac his son; and he split wood for the burnt offering, and arose and went to the place of which God had told him." He was absolutely obedient to the Father.

> Abraham had to make the choice and recognize who truly came first in his life.

Of course, Scripture only reports what Abraham *did*—not what he *felt*. We are not privy to the turmoil, heartache, and struggle he experienced, though we know how excruciating it must have been for him to carry out the Lord's commands. Surely the thought of having to bind his boy and sacrifice him as a burnt offering became more real and more painful with every step. No doubt he hoped that the loving Lord who had made him the promise—the One who, after twenty-five years of waiting, had given him this beloved son—had a greater plan (Heb. 11:17–19).

I can only imagine that he recalled all the wonderful moments he and Isaac had enjoyed together. The day Isaac was born. The moment he took his first step. The first time this beautiful child threw his arms around Abraham's neck and said, "Daddy, I love you!" All those mornings they'd walked together—Abraham patiently teaching Isaac how to care for the land and livestock. All those nights they sat side-by-side, looking at the stars and talking about God's promises. Soon, all of it would be no more. His precious boy would be gone.

Undoubtedly, submitting to the Lord's command was not easy for this godly man. In fact, we can be certain it was downright agonizing. And though we do not know what Abraham thought, we do know what he did. *He obeyed anyway*. He took his son and wood for the burnt offering and made his way to Mount Moriah. He acknowledged that the Lord is God. And he embraced the principle that would ultimately be verbalized by Job, "The LORD gave and the LORD has taken away. Blessed be the name of the LORD" (Job 1:21). And God blessed Abraham because of it.

WHO OR WHAT IS ON THE THRONE OF YOUR HEART?

Obeying the Lord may not be easy for you, either. It may be extremely difficult to submit to His timing, His ways, and His commands—just as it was for Abraham and Sarah. But, friend, it is absolutely necessary. Why? Because He is GOD and honoring anything before Him is *idolatry*, which is condemned repeatedly throughout Scripture (Ex. 20:3–5; Lev. 19:4, 26:1; Isa. 42:17, 44:9; Ezek. 5:11; 1 Cor. 10:13–14; Gal. 5:19–21; and 1 John 5:21, to name a few). The Father will not have any rivals for your affection. He wants to come first and have priority in your life—just as He did in Abraham's life.

We do not use the term *idol* much anymore, and certainly, of the Ten Commandments, the one we probably contemplate least is the first, "I am the LORD your God . . . you shall have no other gods before Me" (Ex. 20:2–3). As modern believers, we generally do not consider idolatry a problem for us, because we usually think of it as constructing and worshiping deities of wood, clay, stone, and other materials—such as when Aaron made the golden calf for the Israelites (Ex. 32).

But there is far more to idolatry than merely fashioning statues. Idolatry is a stronghold that slips stealthily into your life, and you may not even know it is there. This is why the apostle Paul admonishes in Colossians 3:5, "Consider the members of your earthly body as dead to immorality, impurity, passion, evil desire, and greed, which amounts to idolatry." Because he understood that an idol is anything that you value more—either by your attitude or actions—than God. It competes for your love and devotion to Him. It causes you to doubt, avoid, and even forget Him. You may not even realize how crucial it has become to you because its lure is so subtle and deceptive, but you protect it because it has come to represent your worth and security.

> An idol is anything that you value more—either by your attitude or actions—than God.

Therefore, I ask you to examine your heart and see if you have any of the indicators that there might be a problem.

1. Do you spend your time and energy trying to figure out what will happen, even though God has instructed you to trust Him and lean not on your own understanding? Do you find it difficult to fix your focus on Him rather than the object of your desire?

2. Are you trying to "help" God with the situation—engineering your own ways of overcoming obstacles and revealing your lack of faith in His provision? Are you frustrated and disheartened by how your circumstances look, though the Father assures you daily that He is making a way for you?

3. When it seems as if you will lose the object of your desire or that a particular option is closed to you, do you lash out at God, angry that He is not giving you what you want? Does that loss turn your heart against the Lord?

Are any of these true for you? Is it possible that you have something in your life that you care about more than you care about the Father?

Your first inclination may be to deny it. In fact, I think most people would respond, "No. There's nothing more important to me than the Lord. He's the only One I pray to. Yes, I'm trying to figure this situation out, but that's harmless. After all, doesn't Scripture say, 'God helps those who help themselves'?" I want to be clear: That saying did *not* come from the Bible, neither is it a scriptural principle.[5] The Father blesses *obedience* (Jer. 7:23) and *godly discipline* (1 Tim. 4:7–8), not human wisdom (Prov. 14:12) and self-reliance (James 4:13–15).

But as believers it is sometimes very difficult to admit we have surrendered our hearts over to something other than our Savior. In fact, everything in us may fight against it. This is for three reasons.

1. We want to believe we're good enough to merit our salvation and the blessings God gives us.

Out of pride, we want to measure up to what we think Jesus expects of us and earn His favor. So to confess there are strongholds or idols in our lives would mean admitting we are not perfect—not deserving of His goodness, but dependent upon His loving-kindness and grace (Eph. 2:8–9).

However, it is extremely important for you to understand that there is wonderful freedom in admitting your sinfulness and allowing the Lord to cleanse you of unrighteousness (1 John 1:9). Accepting His forgiveness and resting in the joy it brings is life at its best. So stop struggling with whether or not you are worthy of the blessing and accept His all-sufficient forgiveness. Allow Him to free you from any idols in your heart. Humble yourself before Him because He promises He will lift you up (James 4:10).

2. We realize that admitting we have strongholds means acknowledging we need to change.

Many of us are afraid to allow the Lord to transform our lives (Rom. 12:1–2). Why? Because doing so would mean giving up ungodly thought patterns and behaviors and confronting wounds and beliefs that we've held since childhood. To do so may also require us to relinquish the desires we long for or the possessions we depend upon for security. Therefore, we prefer to live in the same defeated status quo than to experience the extraordinary life God has planned for us.

Certainly, it is a discipline to let go—it's not easy for anyone. Our fleshly nature holds on and opposes the liberating work of the Holy Spirit within us at every turn (Rom. 8:6–17). Even so, when you allow Him to change you and lead you on the path of His will, you will experience joyous liberty and assurance. Be confident that if the Father asks you to surrender something, it is because He has something better for you. He is always faithful to guard whatever you entrust to Him (2 Tim. 1:12).

3. We are trying to meet a need that only God can fulfill.

The truth of the matter is that the object or person we want always represents more to us than what they actually are. For example, I have often seen people turn down employment even though they needed to put food on the table and pay the bills. Why? Because they were looking for occupations that represented their education, status in society, and success. They wanted jobs that fulfilled their inherent need to feel respected, worthwhile, and capable. In other words, they tried to find their identity in their profession rather than in Christ and may not have even fully realized it.

Perhaps Abraham struggled with some of the same issues. Yes, he wanted a son he could love and raise, but he also wanted someone to carry on his name and heritage. Thankfully, because Abraham saw that his fundamental legacy and worth were in the Lord—not Isaac—he was able to obey God with a fully devoted and faithful heart.

Ultimately, you must decide the same. The needs you have for love, respect, security, admiration, or what have you, cannot be met by the desire of your heart. They are fulfilled by God—and Him alone.

COMMON IDOLS

The needs you have for love, respect, security, and admiration cannot be met by the desire of your heart. They are fulfilled by God—and Him alone.

So what is it that you need to deal with? Remember, an idol is a stronghold that is very subtle. It steals into your life covertly, roots itself in your emotions, and becomes more important to you than God. It keeps you from looking to Him for your worth and security.

No one can identify an idol in your life except the Lord—and He sees your heart very clearly. For example, Abraham was a very rich man, so it is interesting that God did not say, "Take all your sheep, goats, and camels and sacrifice them to Me." But they did not have a hold on his heart. There was only one thing that competed with Abraham's total devotion to Him. And that was Isaac.

What is it in you? The Father is faithful to show you if an idol exists, but be very careful you don't rationalize away what He reveals to you. It is easy to say, "God, You don't really care about that; it's not important"—especially if He brings up an issue you do not expect. But remember, only the Lord knows if you have an idol and what it is. So if He puts His finger on something in your life, set your heart to deal with it immediately.

Some common things we often hold too tightly to are:

OUR OWN UNDERSTANDING

As we discussed earlier, what often makes us lose our focus on the Father is that we don't understand what is going on or why He would allow us to face so much adversity. Certain puzzle pieces are missing. Our minds cannot fully comprehend what's happening, so we repeatedly analyze the situation—scrutinizing it incessantly from every angle we can conceive. In a practical sense, we act as if we are omniscient about the struggles we face and we pretend to control our circumstances, thereby maintaining a false sense of security.

Sadly, when events don't proceed the way we expect, we are left discouraged, disillusioned, and with even deeper feelings of insecurity. Don't fall into that trap. God unmistakably commands you: trust Him and don't rely on your understanding (Prov. 3:5–6). I tell you this with full certainty: You do not and cannot know all the details about your situation. But the Father does.

> I tell you this with full certainty: You do not and cannot know all the details about your situation. But the Father does.

Remember, an idol is anything that you trust through your actions or attitude more than you trust God. So if your comprehension of the situation is causing you to doubt the Lord, then your own understanding has become an idol. You are choosing your ability to understand over the Father.

But the Lord is clear, "My thoughts are not your thoughts, nor are your ways My ways . . . For as the heavens are higher than the earth, so are My ways higher than your ways and My thoughts than your thoughts" (Isa. 55:8–9). In other words, He accomplishes His purposes in a far different manner than you do.

Friend, we all want to understand what God is doing in our lives. It does not make sense to us that He would make us wait, put so many obstacles in our path, and deny us something that is so crucial to our lives and happiness. But this is no reason to reject Him. On the contrary, it is reason to depend on Him all the more and diligently seek His good purposes.

So when everything appears to contradict what the Father has promised you, remember that your perspective of the situation is incomplete and that your trust in Him is more essential than ever. Say, "I don't understand this, but God does. I do not see all that is happening, but the Lord is working on my behalf in the unseen." And though everything within you may fight against it, remain faithful, virtuous, obedient, self-controlled, loving, and above all, exhibit faith in His unfailing character.

A SENSE OF SECURITY

Another idol that we struggle with is our own security—whether we receive it through our wealth, employment, power, social influence, the government, physical strength, beauty, intelligence, or what have you. We don't like being out of control or trusting our future to One we do not see. Rather, we prefer a steady stream of income, reliable resources, and predictable results. So when we are forced to wait, see our bills pile up, or encounter threats that challenge our sense of well-being, we do not like it and begin to distrust the Father.

Of course, you may say, "But isn't that normal? Shouldn't I plan for tomorrow and be responsible?" Having goals can be very good and godly—as long as you are seeking the Lord's guidance. But often, what we are really seeking is to create security by our own means rather than depending on God. This is what happened with the nation of Israel and was the original reason that idols were so tempting to them.

You see, throughout Israel's early history, its success or failure hinged on two short rainy seasons (Deut. 11:14). The early rains, which occurred in the fall, would soften the ground for planting and nourish the seeds. The late rains replenished the crops before the summer heat and sustained them through the harvest. Everything depended on the precipitation—if it was abundant, there would be plenty of produce. If it were sparse, there would be famine and devastation. Even today, water is a crucial commodity to the Israeli economy and much of their outstanding technology has been developed to make the most of their water supply.

But during biblical times, the Israelites had no such innovation to ensure successful harvests. In fact, when they were about to enter the Promised Land, Moses said to them, "The land into which you are about to cross to possess it, a land of hills and valleys, *drinks water from the rain of heaven*, a land for which the LORD your God cares" (Deut. 11:11–12, emphasis added). In other words, they were to plant and depend completely on the Father for their yield.

But that didn't stop the Israelites from trying to find an easier way to live (Jer. 5:23–25). Because these two short periods of rainfall in the Promised Land were so important, the Israelites were always anxious about whether or not there was going to be enough water for their crops—and sufficient produce for survival. So instead of trusting God to provide for them, the Israelites turned to the rain and fertility deities of their neighbors, thinking they'd have a better yield.

Perhaps you recall reading about the prophet Elijah on Mount Carmel who said, "How long will you hesitate between two opinions? If the LORD is God, follow Him; but if Baal, follow him" (1 Kings 18:21). Baal was the Canaanite deity of the storm, who supposedly controlled the rain for the harvest. The Israelites had begun to trust him for their needs, rather than the Lord God, who had always sustained them.

So in order to reveal who was truly providing for them, Elijah challenged Baal's prophets to call out to their deity and bid him to send fire from heaven to consume an offering. Elijah would then call out to the Lord God, asking the same. Whoever responded— whether Baal or the Lord—would prove to be the rightful, unquestionable God and the actual source of their supply.

> The Lord, the one true God, faithfully answered Elijah's call—just as He always does for all of His children.

Of course, Baal never made a peep. This was because Baal was not real—he was merely a man-made idol, a creation of their imaginations intended to foster a sense of security that was ultimately false (Ps. 115:4–7). But the Lord, the one true God, faithfully answered Elijah's call—just as He always does for all of His children (1 Kings 18:21–40).

This is why the prophet Jeremiah said, "Are there any among the idols of the nations who give rain? Or can the heavens grant showers? Is it not You, O LORD our God? Therefore we hope in You, for You are the one who has done all these things" (14:22). Only the Lord God can reliably provide all we need. He is our only real security.

But you see, the Israelite's idolatry occurred because they wanted assurance in their daily life issues beyond what God offered. We do the same. And like them, we are geared to trust the provision we can observe and touch with our hands. But just like with Baal, whatever we build our security on other than the Lord will eventually fail us. It's not real (Matt. 7:24–27). We can lose our wealth, our jobs, our power, our social standing—but we will never, ever lose the Lord our God. He will never leave or forsake us (Deut. 31:8).

Therefore, friend, if the impediment to focusing on the Father is your need for tangible security—if this has become your idol—then I would point you to the testimony of the prophet Habakkuk, who had a heart of genuine faith. He understood Who was really feeding and sustaining him when he said:

> Though the fig tree should not blossom
> And there be no fruit on the vines,
> Though the yield of the olive should fail
> And the fields produce no food,
> Though the flock should be cut off from the fold
> And there be no cattle in the stalls,
> Yet I will exult in the LORD,
> I will rejoice in the God of my salvation.
> The Lord GOD is my strength,
> And He has made my feet like hinds' feet,
> And makes me walk on my high places. (Hab. 3:17–19)

Habakkuk names all the major crops and sources of food in the region and says that, even if they all fail, God is still worthy of praise because He is our true strength and supply. And as we saw when the Lord provided the manna to the Israelites as they made the exodus from Egypt (Exod. 16), when the oil and flour didn't run out for the widow of Zarephath (1 Kings 17:8–17), and when Jesus fed five thousand people with just five loaves and two fish (Matt. 14:15–21), He is able to provide for us supernaturally even when everything else we see disappoints.

GOALS AND DREAMS

Our aspirations can also impede us from making God our primary focus. We become so driven to achieve our objectives and daily goals that we forget the eternal life we have been given (John 17:3) and all the good things the Lord has purposed for us to accomplish (Eph. 2:20). Our dreams become an idol—more important than what the Father desires to do in and through us.

This reminds me of a parable Jesus told of an ambitious man whose land was very fruitful. Sadly, this man was so consumed with what he wanted to attain that he lost sight of what was important. Jesus explained,

> "He began reasoning to himself, saying, 'What shall I do, since I have no place to store my crops?' Then he said, 'This is what I will do: I will tear down my barns and build larger ones, and there I will store all my grain and my goods. And I will say to my soul, "Soul, you have many goods laid up for many years to come; take your ease, eat, drink and be merry." ' " (Luke 12:17–19)

In other words, this man sought to build his own kingdom and contentment. Unfortunately, he made two terrible mistakes as he made his plans. First, he was focused on "me," "myself," and "I"—he never considered anyone beyond himself. Everything he was amassing was for his own benefit and pleasure, and he didn't make any effort to alleviate the suffering of those in desperate need (Matt. 25:34–41).

But his second error was that he never looked beyond this life to the one to come. Look at what Luke 12:17 says: "He began reasoning to himself." This man did not seek the Lord's wisdom or guidance. He did not ask the Father what he should pursue. Rather, he did what was right in his own eyes and did not consider himself as accountable to anyone (Ps. 10:4).

In a practical sense, he said, "In his heart, 'There is no God' " (Ps. 14:1). And we know how Scripture refers to that attitude—it is very unwise. So Jesus explained, "God said to him, 'You fool! This very night your soul is required of you; and now who will own what you have prepared?' " (Luke 12:20).

Sadly, many people fail to consider eternity or God's will. They focus on this life, which is "just a vapor that appears for a little while and then vanishes away" (James 4:14), instead of on the life that is to come, which endures forever (1 John 2:17).

Because of this, a friend of mine—an elderly man who was very wise—asked his grandson what he planned to do with his life.

The young man replied, "I'm going to study and be educated. I'm going to find a trade that fits my abilities, talents, and skills."

The grandfather nodded and said, "What then?"

"Well, I'll work diligently and try to make a name for myself—so I can make a difference in the world."

The grandfather again inquired, "Okay. What then?"

"I suppose I will try to save my money—accumulate a healthy nest egg so I can have some ease as I grow older. So I can retire and just enjoy life when I am your age."

Again the grandfather questioned, "All right. What then?"

Frustrated, the young man answered, "Well then after that, I guess I'll die!"

The elderly gentleman looked into his grandson's face with love and compassion and one more time asked, "What then?"

To many, this young man's plan probably sounds reasonable, but his grandfather knew better. When our earthly lives come to an end, we must all be prepared to give an account to the Lord (Rom. 14:12). But too many people arrive at retirement with their wealth, titles, achievements, reputation, or what have you, and completely forget to prepare for what comes next. And in all my years of doing funerals, I have never seen a casket filled with real estate deeds, stock certificates, university degrees, or anything like that. Why? Because you cannot take it with you. But what you have done in obedience to the Father will endure unto eternity (Heb. 6:10).

This is why Jesus said, "Do not store up for yourselves treasures on earth, where moth and rust destroy, and where thieves break in and steal. But store up for yourselves treasures in heaven, where neither moth nor rust destroys, and where thieves do not break in or steal; for where your treasure is, there your heart will be also" (Matt. 6:19–21).

> What you have done in obedience to the Father will endure unto eternity.

In other words, if your dreams and goals are coming between you and the Father, it is time to rethink your priorities. Make sure you are pouring your heart, soul, mind, and strength into what will last forever. And be assured, your Lord God "is a rewarder of those who seek Him" (Heb. 11:6).

RELATIONSHIPS

Of course, as we saw in Abraham's life, sometimes certain relationships become an idol—relationships that you have or desire to engage in. Perhaps you wish to have a child as he and Sarah did, or maybe you have been asking God for a spouse. It may even be a loved one who has drifted away from you that you long to have back or a situation that never seems to improve.

So as you wait upon God and look to Him for guidance, this despair overwhelms you. No matter how much you attempt to focus on the Father, your attention returns to this person or group of people. Feelings of rejection, fear, lack of self-worth, or bitterness continue to arise because of your circumstances. And ultimately, they drive you away from God, not toward Him. The Lord tries to move you in a certain direction, but you find yourself resisting Him because of how it may impact your relationship. Your desire for these relationships and the influence of the people you wish to please become impediments to doing His will.

This does not mean your loved ones should not be significant to you. They absolutely should. When the Lord was going to destroy the wicked cities of Sodom and Gomorrah where Abraham's nephew Lot was residing, Abraham did all he could to save him (Gen. 18:17–33). We should pray for our friends and family members, and minister to them in whatever ways are good and appropriate. However, they should never be more important to us than God is—which sadly becomes the case for many people.

For example, I recall one gentleman I spoke with several years ago who was desperate to marry, but it was obvious from the way he interacted with his fiancée that marrying her would be a terrible mistake. So I told him, "You are entering into a relationship that is not the will of God. I'm pleading with you—don't do it. Don't jump into this. You are going to regret it."

He replied, "Charles, I hear what you're saying, but I'm going to do it anyway. I just need to be married. God will understand."

That matrimony lasted only six weeks. But the destruction it caused endured a great deal longer.

Unfortunately, this is the situation for many singles—especially as they grow older. I've seen men and women alike reach their thirties and forties and begin to panic, afraid they will never meet the right person. All the while, they are thinking, *If I could just get married, I would be so happy.* They yearn to have *someone*—anyone—in their lives, which subsequently clouds their ability to make wise decisions.

Certainly, many of the Christian singles I've known over the years would acknowledge that, in theory, no person can meet all their needs. They would agree that only God can satisfy their deepest longings. But how they act is a different matter. And when they meet another person who is willing to tie the knot, I've sadly seen many of them rush into the union without much discernment. They don't consult the Father, ensuring that this is the person He has in mind for them. Their prayers are based on keeping their boyfriend or girlfriend happy, rather than seeking God's will. Ultimately, however, they want just one thing—and that's to ease their loneliness. Now, what they're really longing for is true intimacy—genuine oneness of heart and spirit that the Father intended for the marriage relationship. But because they are tired of waiting, they settle for sex and a false sense of security. And what they reap are problems and devastating heartbreak.

Friend, if this is you, do not sell yourself short. Don't rush into a bad relationship because of fear or loneliness. You've waited a long time, and I am certain it's probably been very difficult. But when you are entering into a commitment that will affect the rest of your life, the wisest course of action is always to wait upon the Father and seek His guidance. I've known many extraordinary people who waited patiently for the Lord and married very happily later in life. And God blessed them with very joyful, successful marriages because of their obedience and willingness to live by His schedule.

Of course, this is not the only way our relationships can become idols and impede our fellowship with the Lord. There are literally hundreds of ways our interactions with others can become a stumbling block in our relationship with God if we are not focused on Him. So no matter what person or group of people are causing you to distrust, ignore, or even forget the Father, it is absolutely crucial that you seek Him, release those others to Him, and allow Him to put those connections in their proper place. This is the only way you will be able to enjoy the deep and meaningful intimacy, worth, and acceptance you have been longing for.

THE PAST

Now, this leads us to one of the most destructive potential idols of all— the past. Present relationships can become an impediment to our relationship with God, but so can the ones we've experienced in years gone by if people have hurt us, if we harbor unforgiveness, or if we allow the unkind treatment of others to shape how we see the Father.

The truth is, we have all been wounded by other people. We've all faced difficult and heartbreaking trials. And when terrible things happen, the human response is to wonder why the Father allowed us to suffer. Perhaps we even feel some initial confusion in our hearts toward Him because He didn't protect us or stop the situation that injured us so profoundly. But there is a dangerous point when our pain turns to bitterness and unforgiveness. In that moment, we begin to feel we cannot really trust God, and we identify those agonizing experiences as proof that we can't rely upon Him. We become suspicious of the Lord, fearfully expecting that He will send another trial or wound us further.

Perhaps that is where you are today and why you're having so great a difficulty trusting the Father. Maybe someone abused you terribly or someone very dear to you has passed away. It may be that you've made some mistake and feel as if you are no longer acceptable to the Father. It could even be that you cried out to God for His help in a crucial situation in your life, but it deteriorated anyway. You wonder, *What point is there in trusting Him and waiting on Him when He permitted this to happen?*

> If you live gripping the past, you will forfeit your future. Adversity can either make you bitter or better.

Friend, I don't know why the Lord allowed you to suffer in the manner He did. But I do know one thing for certain—if you live gripping the past, you will forfeit your future. I've seen it repeatedly throughout my life—adversity can either make you bitter or better.

This reminds me of a fine young fellow I had the privilege to work with some years ago. From the outside, it seemed as if he had everything going for him—he was handsome, gifted, and very charming. Sadly, he couldn't see any of that. Internally, he was full of pain, unworthiness, and turmoil.

The problem started when he was nine years old. His parents were arguing about him in the next room, and he overheard the destructive words that absolutely shattered his young heart, "Why should I care about him? I don't want him!" You and I can imagine how painful it would be for a child to hear such a statement from the very people who were supposed to love and nurture him. Even worse, he began to believe that God felt the same way. I saw the Father working in his life, showing him His great love, and providing opportunity after opportunity to correct this erroneous belief that he was unwanted. But this young man just couldn't allow the Father to heal this painful wound. His past became an idol—he trusted his experience more than he believed in God.

Regrettably, he never let those words go, and they drove how he related to every aspect of his life from then on. He longed to feel respected and worthy—as if he were somebody. Every goal he pursued—education, family, power, etc.—was so he could fill the horrible void in his life. But none of it did. Instead, those awful words, "Why should I care about him? I don't want him," tormented him every day of his life. Eventually, after a series of painful events, that dear young man ended his life—absolutely devastating everyone who knew him.

Friend, don't let this happen to you. You don't have to allow the past to rob you of all the blessings God has for you. On the contrary, the adversity you've faced can be a bridge to a deeper relationship with the Father, if you will set your heart to trust Him. You have the power to choose how you will react to what you experience and whether it will defeat or develop you.

In fact, this young man's story lies in stark contrast to the testimony of another person I know—one who demonstrated quite a different response to her painful past. When this lady was in her teens, her mother had a terrible automobile accident that kept her in the hospital for a year and a half. There were so many complications from the accident that the family did not know from day to day whether they would lose her. In fact, on several occasions, the doctors told them to prepare a gravesite. Thankfully, the mother survived her initial injuries, though she would require a great deal of care for the rest of her life.

However, the stress of the situation ended up being too much for the girl's stepfather, so he served the mother with divorce papers while she was still in critical condition. The girl and her mother were completely devastated. Not only were both their futures altered forever by that accident, but also the one person who had promised to be there for them "in sickness and in health, until death do us part" was gone. They felt profound helplessness, hopelessness, and rejection.

You can imagine the resentment this could have stirred up in this young lady and how this could have negatively shaped her perception of God. But after more than two decades of caring for her disabled mother, there's no evidence of bitterness in her—she always has a smile on her face.

When I asked her about how she overcame the situation and forgave her stepfather, she quoted 1 John 4:20: "If someone says, 'I love God,' and hates his brother, he is a liar; for the one who does not love his brother whom he has seen, cannot love God whom he has not seen." Then she said, "It took some time, but I decided I wanted to really love God—I wanted to believe Him and His Word. And to do that, I had to forgive my stepfather; I couldn't continue to harbor resentment toward him. I also had to trust that if the Lord permitted all of that to happen to us, then He would bring good from it—just like He promises in Romans 8:28. And He has! It's just like you always say, Dr. Stanley. God doesn't allow anything in our lives unless somehow it will ultimately work for His glory and our benefit."

> No matter what you've endured, the Lord can work through it to cultivate your character and fulfill His purposes for your life.

In other words, this lady didn't allow her past to become an idol. She chose to believe the Father, and He has used the situation to give her a ministry, purpose, and great joy (2 Cor. 1:3–7). No matter what you've endured, the Lord can work through it to cultivate your character and fulfill His purposes for your life as well. He will ensure that no trial or tragedy you ever experience—even the long seasons of waiting—will go without some kind of redemption, if you will believe Him and invite His presence in your life.

HOBBIES

Our list of common idols would not be complete if I didn't mention that our hobbies and preferred forms of entertainment might also be competing with our relationship with God. Though pastimes such as sports, shopping, television, exercise, social media, and other interests are not necessarily wrong in themselves, if they have more of your attention than the Lord does, then there is certainly a problem.

For example, I love photography. In fact, I'd rather be taking photographs than doing just about anything else in the world—except preaching and being with God's people, of course. There is just nothing like being out in the wilderness and capturing the images of God's amazing creation—snow-capped mountains, crystal-blue lakes, brightly colored birds, brilliantly arrayed flowers, you name it. I am in awe of the Father's awesome power to form such incredible beauty and how He so carefully crafts every detail.

But I recall a time when God directed me to release this beloved pastime. You see, the Lord led us to purchase some property for the church, and we needed funds. As pastor, I felt I should set the example of sacrifice and commitment that I was asking of the congregation, so I began to pray about what the Father wanted me to give. Almost immediately, I was moved to sell the family automobile and travel trailer and give the money to the building fund.

Naturally, I thought that was enough. But the Lord spoke to my heart and said, "Charles, you've never offered Me anything but money." Suddenly, my thoughts turned to my cameras, and I knew that the Father wanted me to release them to Him.

I confess that my first thought was, *Oh no, Lord. Why would You want my cameras—the one hobby I enjoy? You're asking too much.*

But I knew what I had to do. I had to decide what was more

important to me—my Savior or photography. And when I asked myself, "Is my heart tied up in my cameras or in what the Lord is doing at the church?"—there was only one answer I could live with.

So the next day, I gathered all my equipment and handed it over to a friend who bought and sold used gear. Then I gave the money to the building fund. It seemed as if I had done everything the Father required of me.

But somewhere inside me, I could sense that something wasn't quite right. I missed my equipment. Deep down, I wanted it back and was grieving the loss. It was then that Matthew 6:21 came to mind, "Where your treasure is, there your heart will be also." I realized that emotionally, I was still holding on to them. I had not really surrendered the gear completely. So in prayer, I chose God as my treasure over photography. I turned the equipment over to Him in my heart and thanked Him for the opportunity to make the sacrifice out of love for Him. It was not easy, but I was immediately aware of His awesome presence and comfort.

Now, you may be thinking, *Why wouldn't God want you to have a hobby? Doesn't He want us to enjoy life?* Of course He does. But when you and I prioritize anything over our relationships with the Lord, He views it as competition. So He will target it in order to stop it from interfering with our fellowship with Him. And the truth of the matter is, even "harmless" hobbies and pastimes can consume us. How many people have missed worshiping God on Sundays because they prefer weekends at the lake or on the golf course? How many have chosen to invest money in their shopping habit rather than give a tithe? And how many would elect to read posts on social media rather than have a meaningful quiet time with the Father? The choices may appear insignificant, but they can have a harmful cumulative effect on your relationship with Him.

Of course, sometimes what a person spends time on is outright destructive—such as addictive behaviors like substance abuse, gambling, and sexual sins. Although these activities may promise immediate pleasure without penalty, there are always devastating consequences for engaging in them. Why? Because they are all intended to dull some deep pain that only God can heal or placate a need that only He can satisfy. And as we said before, any time we attempt to meet our needs apart from the Lord, we sin.

Friend, if you are engaging in an addictive pastime, you have a very dangerous idol in your life and are experiencing ever-growing relational separation from the Lord every time you participate in it. I realize that you may be using your hobby to diminish profound feelings of agony, emptiness, shame, worthlessness, fear, failure, or dishonor, but this is not the way to go about it. Addictive activities deepen those emotions by taking you further from the Father—the only One who can truly forgive you and give you the love and worth you long for. The more you engage in these behaviors, the more bondage you experience and the less they dull your pain or provide you with pleasure—even briefly. You may think you can handle it, but friend, that addiction is really controlling you. It is a terribly vicious cycle that can only end in destruction (Prov. 16:25).

The good news is that no matter how far you've strayed from God, it only takes one step to get back to Him (1 John 1:9). So do not ignore what He is speaking to your heart at this moment. Turn to the Father, confess what you've done, and express your desire for His help to overcome your destructive habits. Do not allow feelings of shame or embarrassment to keep you from returning to Him. He loves you just the way you are, and Jesus' sacrifice on the cross covers all of your sin (Eph. 2:3–5). There is hope for you! He can and will restore you. Do not fight Him any longer—allow Him to heal you.

> The good news is that no matter how far you've strayed from God, there is only one step back to Him.

LETTING GO

As you read through this list of common idols, did any of them strike a chord within you? Is God calling anything to mind? As we've seen, the basis of Abraham's struggle was the *priority* he placed on the desire of his heart. So what is it that comes first in your life? Is there anything that takes precedence over what the Lord wants for you? Are there any relationships, possessions, goals, pastimes, or what have you, that you would have trouble letting go of if God asked you to surrender them? How about if He didn't ask—you just lost them? Would you be so furious with the Father that you would run from Him?

What do you look to for security—and what would you do if that vanished? Is there anything that could be taken from you that would ultimately motivate you to give up on the Lord altogether?

Likewise, is there anything you are choosing over God on a daily basis? For example, rather than spending time with Him, are you filling your moments with work, hobbies, social media, entertainment, or people? Are there any activities or behaviors you refuse to relinquish, even though you know they hinder your relationship with Him? Are there people or situations that influence you to do what you know would displease Him?

> Your idol will continue to cause you undue pain and fracture your relationship with the Father until you surrender it.

How about that heart's desire you've been waiting for? Have you fixated on one option, regardless of how the Father has directed you? Do you continue to wrestle with Him—insisting He answer your prayers in the way you demand, rather than doing what He wants? Would you accept it if God said no or if He instructed you to take your hands off the situation?

Friend, it may be very frightening for you to surrender your idol—it is for everyone. But understand, it will continue to cause you undue pain and fracture your relationship with the Father until you do. You may miss the best God has planned if you refuse to lay it down.

So how do we give up our idols? We know it is possible because of the promise we are given in 1 Corinthians 10:13–14, "No temptation has overtaken you but such as is common to man; and God is faithful, who will not allow you to be tempted beyond what you are able, but with the temptation will provide the way of escape also, so that you will be able to endure it. Therefore, my beloved, flee from idolatry." The Lord can help you escape from the bondage of that idol in your life. How does He do so?

1. The Father will help you recognize that He is not first in your life.
If you recall, in Chapter 1, we discussed the fact that God often uses times of waiting to sift our motives and reveal our sin to us. It is amazing how all of our doubts, insecurities, and strongholds surface when He seems to delay—we can tell where the bondage is in our lives by the questions we ask Him and the fears we wrestle with.

So that you can let go of your idol, agree with God that you have a problem. Don't try to blame others or your circumstances for its existence or control over you; rather, take responsibility for allowing that desire to be more important to you than the Lord. Acknowledge that you've permitted that idol in your life—and that you've willingly chosen to spend more of your time and energy thinking about it than Him. Then ask the Father to help you make Him first.

2. The Lord will help you discern which thoughts are causing you to stumble and how much of your time and energy you're putting into your idol.
You see, your dependence on that idol begins with what you think. Though your thoughts may appear innocent or harmless, they trigger a pattern of deliberation that eventually leads to a disbelief in God's love and provision. So you find a way to meet your needs because you don't trust Him to satisfy them for you.

For example, when the Israelites left Egypt and were wandering in the wilderness, we know that they made this stark and terrible statement, "Would that we *had died* by the Lord's hand in the land of Egypt, when we sat by the pots of meat, when we ate bread to the full; for you have brought us out into this wilderness *to kill this whole assembly* with hunger" (Exod. 16:3, emphasis added). Did they really prefer dying in Egypt? Did they genuinely believe Moses' goal was to kill them with hunger? How could they possibly come to such conclusions—especially since they were slaves in Egypt and Moses had risked his life to deliver them? And why was death the only outcome they could conceive of—either perishing in Egypt or starving in the wilderness? Exodus 16:1 tells us it was "the fifteenth day of the second month after their departure from the land of Egypt"—and none of them had yet died from starvation.

But we must understand that their reasoning did not begin at that point. More than likely, they began by thinking something as simple as *I wonder when we're going to eat?* or, *You know what would be great right now, some of that bread we used to enjoy when we were in Goshen.* These are innocent thoughts. However, left unchecked, they activated a series of deliberations that—for the Israelites—ended with death.

The same is true for you. There are certain questions and phrases that arise in your mind that begin your downhill slide to doubt and disbelief. You may not even realize they are there, but the Father can identify them for you. Likewise, He can convict you of all the ways you are investing your time and energy in feeding those destructive thoughts and the activities that accompany them. He can also teach you how to turn them around and use them to build your faith, rather than destroy it.

For example, when the Israelites wondered about where their next meal would come from, their thoughts naturally took an undesirable turn. But what if instead of being negative, they had focused on the Father's astounding provision on their behalf? How the God who sent the plagues to liberate them from slavery, who parted the Red Sea, who defeated Pharaoh and his armies, who led them by a pillar of cloud by day and fire by night—how their wonderful Deliverer would certainly sustain them. No doubt that focused on His provision, they would have been filled with faith.

Likewise, the Father can change how you view your situation. Just remember, it ultimately comes down to control. You will try to figure out and engineer your path when you do not trust Him to direct your steps. So you must decide to have faith in His provision. You will not be able to dislodge your idol until you do.

So examine your heart. When the Lord seems to delay, what questions and fears do you wrestle with? Do you feel that God is unreliable? Where do your feelings of distrust toward Him originate? And what are you choosing to depend upon instead of Him? Write down your thoughts, take them to the Father, and invite Him to free you from any bondage that may be causing them. Replace the erroneous beliefs you hold with His truth. In doing so, you "demolish arguments and every pretension that sets itself up against the knowledge of God, and . . . take captive every thought to make it obedient to Christ" (2 Cor. 10:5, NIV).

3. God can help you put Him first in your life and arrange all other priorities in a manner that will honor Him.

God does this through the prompting of His Holy Spirit. When you must make a decision or feel anxious, the Father reminds you to seek Him and experience the great peace of being in His wonderful presence. Instead of succumbing to the emotions of anger, fear, sorrow, or the like, they become indicators of your need to return to His throne of grace.

Of course, you may be thinking, *Well, I can't just read Scripture and pray all the time.* No one is saying that's what you must do. Rather, it means that you actively involve the Lord in your life and direct your thoughts to Him even when pressures and obstacles are competing for your attention.

Remember, one of my goals in this book is to get you to change your focus from the blessings you long for to the One who bestows them—to "set your mind on the things above, not on the things that are on earth" (Col. 3:2). And to "not be conformed to this world, but be transformed by the renewing of your mind, so that you may prove what the will of God is, that which is good and acceptable and perfect" (Rom. 12:2). It is only by the guidance of the Holy Spirit that this is possible. Only He knows what is really causing you to cling to those idols. And only He has the power to break their hold over your life. But you must be willing to submit to Him.

4. The Father helps you to understand that it is discipline—not just desire—that determines your victory over idols.
From the beginning, it's important to realize that there's no quick fix for the issues that have constructed a stronghold in your life. Yes, the Father immediately begins giving you the victory—you should not doubt that. But you most likely have been depending on the idol in one form or another for years, and it takes the Holy Spirit time to unearth all the ways it is keeping you bound.

For example, the Lord may immediately deliver someone from a destructive behavior—such as alcoholism or drug use—but He will not stop there. He will continue to work on the underlying issues that caused that addiction in the first place—such as fear, insecurity, unforgiveness, etc. You see, those are the matters that actually keep you stumbling.

Therefore, you must be patient with yourself—giving yourself a chance to form new patterns of thinking as you study God's Word and seek Him in prayer. It takes time and will require endurance, discipline, and determination. But soon enough, the Father will transform your mind—giving you His thoughts, strengthening your faith, and helping you walk in His ways.

Of course, as you're surrendering yourself and your thoughts to Him, it will sometimes mean yielding your expectations for the future to Him as well. That is what makes it difficult. But on the other side of doing so is not only awesome freedom, but God's very best blessings for you—far better than you could possibly ask or imagine (Eph. 3:20). And the fact of the matter is, you don't necessarily lose those things you relinquish to Him— they may be simply repositioned among your priorities. In fact, it's amazing to me how often we get back what we willingly submit to the Lord.

RETURNED

This brings us back to the story of Abraham and Isaac. Upon arriving at Mount Moriah, we know Abraham—out of obedience—bound Isaac and set him on the altar of sacrifice before God (Gen. 22:9). We can just imagine the awful scene—the terrible pain in Abraham's heart and the confused fear in Isaac's eyes.

> It's amazing how often we get back what we willingly submit to the Lord.

But as Abraham's hand rose high in the air, holding the knife that would take Isaac's life, the angel of the Lord appeared to him and made this wonderful declaration, "Abraham, Abraham! . . . Do not stretch out your hand against the lad, and do nothing to him; for now I know that you fear God, since you have not withheld your son, your only son, from Me" (Gen. 22:11–12).

Through his willingness to sacrifice his only son, Abraham showed beyond a shadow of a doubt that the Lord God was his priority. And as often happens, when the Father asks us to give up something important, He is simply confirming to us that He is still first in our lives. And what did Abraham lose by laying down what was most precious to him? Nothing. What did he gain? He got every wonderful blessing the Father had promised him.

That's what happened to me as well. Do you recall how God prompted me to release my cameras to Him? About two months after that happened, a lady I'd never seen before knocked on my door. She had a suitcase and a big sack with her.

"Are you Dr. Stanley?" she asked me.

"Yes, ma'am," I replied.

"Pastor of First Baptist Church?"

"Yes, ma'am."

She said, "Here, these are for you." She then set the suitcase and sack down in front of me and quickly walked off. I didn't even have a chance to ask her any questions. As I looked through the two bags, however, I realized what had happened. God had moved someone in the church to buy every piece of equipment I'd sold—every camera, lens, flash, filter, and accessory—and had it all returned to me.

Now, please understand, I would not have given up all the Father had done in my heart through that experience for the world. My relationship with Him grew by leaps and bounds because He challenged me to establish beyond the shadow of a doubt that He was the first and foremost priority in my life. But to know that He loved me so much that He would restore all of that gear—well, that was absolutely overwhelming. What an astounding blessing! What a loving God!

This is why I can tell you that whatever you release to the Lord, you get more and better in return. I've seen it happen and can say with utmost confidence that you can trust Him completely with anything He asks of you. So open your hands and let your heavenly Father have what you have been holding on to. Because when you invite Him to be number one in your life, the blessings will flow beyond comprehension. And it will make your time of waiting that much easier and more fruitful.

> Whatever you release to the Lord, you get more and better in return.

Father, I love and praise You. How grateful I am that I can depend on You wholeheartedly and for Your liberating work in my life. Thank You for identifying the idols that have been impeding my relationship with You and for helping me to be free of them. My hands and my heart are open to You, Lord Jesus.

Father, I confess the tension and frustration I feel as I wait upon You to answer my prayers. Please forgive me for trying to figure out my own solutions, attempting to "help" You speed up the process, being unwilling to surrender control, and for any way I have placed my desires above You. Lord God, I want You to be first in my life—to trust You completely with my future. I want You to be on the throne of my heart. So Father, please reveal if I am harboring any idols and deliver me from them.

Lord, show me clearly which thoughts are causing me to stumble and how much of my time and energy I am investing in deliberations and activities that do not honor You. Replace my erroneous beliefs with Your wonderful truth. Help me always to put You first and arrange all other priorities in a way that pleases You. And, Lord God, please teach me to be disciplined about seeking You rather than clinging to anything else in the world.

I praise You, Father, because I know beyond a shadow of a doubt that You have my very best interests in mind and that no matter what I release to You, You give me far better in return. Thank You for loving me. In Your holy name I pray, dearest Jesus. Amen.

POINTS FOR ACTIVE WAITING

1. Memorize Proverbs 3:5–6: "Trust in the LORD with all your
   heart and do not lean on your own understanding. In all
   your ways acknowledge Him, and He will make your paths
   straight."

2. Whenever you feel anxious or sorrowful because of what
   you are waiting for, repeat Proverbs 3:5–6, Psalm 27:14, and
   Psalm 62:5–6 to yourself.

3. As suggested in this chapter, write down the thoughts and
   issues that prevent you from focusing on and trusting God,
   and identify what idol(s) they represent in your life. Ask the
   Father to reveal Scripture that counteracts their hold on your
   life. Record the verses and principles He brings to mind in
   the space provided or in your journal. Every time those idols
   surface, confront them with the truth He has given you.

4. Likewise, when your doubtful thoughts and questions come
   to mind, review all the ways the Father helps you overcome
   them (beginning on page 89). Then praise Him for having
   a wonderful plan for your life and giving you the victory in
   your circumstances (Ps. 50:23).

Use this space to respond to the "Points for Active Waiting" and to record prayer requests, key lessons God is teaching you, and your insights about waiting on the Lord to act on your behalf.

It is God who is at work in you,
both to will and to work for His good pleasure.
—Philippians 2:13

{ 4 }

DISCERNING GOD'S WILL
Finding Purpose in the Uncertainty

I think it is safe to say that the questions I am most frequently asked as a pastor involve the issue of God's will. People often inquire, "How do I know what the Lord wants me to do with my life?" Or, "When I have two options, how can I discern which way the Father wants me to go?" I've also found that never are believers so concerned about God's will than during times of waiting—when we desperately want to know what He is up to and whether He will answer our prayers.

After all, we read verses such as 1 John 5:14–15, "This is the confidence which we have before Him, that, if we ask *anything according to His will*, He hears us. And if we know that He hears us in whatever we ask, we know that we have the requests which we have asked from Him" (emphasis added). But how do we ascertain if we are praying according to the Lord's will? Certainly, it would be a great comfort to know we were waiting for something or someone definite—that God's answer to our deepest longings is not an outright, "No!"

For example, David was able to endure through all the adversity because he understood that it was the Lord's plan for him to be king of Israel (1 Sam. 16:1–13). And Abraham was able to be patient because the Father had promised that he would have many descendants and become a great nation (Gen. 12:2). Of course, the delays were extremely difficult for these two men, but they could hold on to the Lord's assurances about their eventual blessings. Unfortunately, the long intervals of anxious anticipation can be even more challenging when you're not really sure where He is taking you or what He's planned for your life.

Perhaps the issue of God's will has been heavy on your heart as you wait for this very reason—you have no idea how He is going to provide for you. You know His plans for you are good, but what are they? Do they really include the fulfillment of your dearest hopes and dreams? Is there any way you can be certain?

> Be assured, the Father *wants* you to know His path for your life.

Friend, please be assured that the Father *wants* you to know His path for your life. In fact, I wholeheartedly believe that if you genuinely desire to follow Him, He will move heaven and earth to show you His will. How can I say this for certain? Because in order for you to accomplish the good goals God has designed for you to achieve, you must know what He has called you to be and do (Eph. 2:10).

Think about it. If you had a son and you wanted him to help with the dishes, would you wait for him to figure out what to do on his own? Of course you wouldn't. First, you would teach your son how to properly wash the dishes and then you would express your expectations about how often you would like for him to carry out his duties. You would direct him carefully. And if he forgot your instructions, you would be sure to remind him.

The same is true for your heavenly Father. He prepares you to do His will, equips you to carry it out, and then He leads you in accomplishing it. It would be completely out of character for Him to hide His plan or refuse to help you achieve it. Instead, the Lord promises, "I will instruct you and teach you in the way which you should go; I will counsel you with My eye upon you" (Ps. 32:8). He wants you to make the right decision. So just like a shepherd lovingly steers a lamb who is prone to wandering, He trains you to listen to His voice, prods you, calls to you, protects you, and even disciplines you in order to lead you in the way you should go (John 10:2–4).

And not only will the Father guide you, but in Jeremiah 29:11–13, which I've shared before, He assures: "I know the plans that I have for you . . . plans for welfare and not for calamity to give you a future and a hope. Then you will call upon Me and come and pray to Me, and I will listen to you. You will seek Me and find Me when you search for Me with all your heart." In other words, you do not have to be afraid that there is only heartbreak ahead. God's purposes for you will bring you contentment, satisfaction, and success. Though you will most likely face times of adversity—as we all do—you can be sure in those seasons that He "causes all things to work together for good to those who love God, to those who are called according to His purpose" (Rom. 8:28). You can be especially confident that He is doing so during this delay—that He is leading you and engineering all circumstances for your ultimate benefit.

UNDERSTANDING THE GOAL

Of course, you may be wondering, *If the Father wants us to know His will and His plans for us are good, why doesn't He just make it all plain? Why all the mystery? Why the tension and pressure? Why does it appear so difficult to determine what He wants?*

Very simply, the reason is that He desires for you to seek Him, and He realizes that adversity and times of waiting motivate you to do so. Yes, He wants to reveal His path for your life to you—that is very important to Him. Yes, having you walk in the center of His will is His goal. But more than anything, the Father wants an intimate, loving relationship with you. So He will delay answering your inquiries about His plans in order to keep your eyes and heart focused on Him.

Recall Jeremiah's words, "You will seek *Me* and find *Me* when you search for *Me* with all your heart" (29:13, emphasis added). His purpose is for you to know *Him*. And when your main objective is to relate to Him personally, intimately, with love and obedience, everything else will fall into place (Isa. 30:20–21).

If you've ever had friends or loved ones who came to you only when they wanted something, perhaps you'll understand His reasons. They were probably nice enough when you would see them, but the only time they asked about how you were feeling or expressed any interest in you was when they required your assistance. They sought you out of convenience, not out of love.

So many of us do the same to God. We only look to Him when we need something, so our relationship with Him is one-sided and stunted in its growth. But the Father does not want to function merely as an impersonal Source of information and provision or a distant Commander shouting instructions. He wants to be involved in our lives in the most profound way, through a relationship that is based on faith and trust.

Perhaps you recall a time when you had to make an important decision and you sought the Lord's direction with all your heart. During that time, not only did you receive His guidance, but you also experienced His goodness, profound presence, and a deep, abiding awareness of who He is and how much He loves you.

I pray you are beginning to see the awesome pattern that arises. God wants you to seek Him, so He allows a need or yearning to surface in your life. You perceive that necessity and pursue His guidance. He delays in His answer so your search for Him will intensify and you will depend on Him more fully. Eventually, He becomes more important to you than the original need—which signifies an important change in the focus of your heart. Finally, He satisfies your longing in a way more wonderful than you could have imagined (Eph. 3:20)—and perhaps far different from how you expected—and by doing so, He reveals Himself to you powerfully. He does all of this to deepen your relationship with Him and develop your capacity to know Him.

God calls you to relationship . . . A need arises . . . You pursue His will . . . You experience a time of waiting . . . Your dependence on God intensifies . . . God reveals Himself to you through His answer.

Friend, you may think that when you pray and while you wait, you are just seeking information from the Father, but throughout that time, He is teaching you to rely upon Him. He is actively working to reveal Himself to you in a more profoundly meaningful way than you've ever known before.

At this point, it would be beneficial to recall the definition we discussed in Chapter 1: Waiting signifies an expectant endurance that is demonstrated by a *directed, purposeful, active,* and *courageous* attitude of prayer. As we saw in the last two chapters, the *directed* aspect of waiting means that our focus is on God, who has the best plan for our lives and is able and willing to help us no matter what we face. He is our steadfast strength and hope during our time of waiting, so we must center our attention on Him if we wish to overcome it successfully.

But we also realize that our waiting is *purposeful*—there is *meaning* in the delay because it trains us to look with anticipation for the Lord's perfect direction, preparation, and provision. In other words, the objective for our waiting is that we learn to seek Him. We know Him better and love Him more because we intentionally and diligently strive to understand and obey His will.

PURPOSE IN GOD'S PLAN

This is the second characteristic of godly prayer in waiting—being *purposeful in pursuing the Lord's plan*—and it is what we'll be examining in this chapter. Instead of looking at our heart's desire as our reason to get out of bed every morning, we find meaning in our lives by discovering the wonderful ways He is leading us day by day and decision by decision.

With this in mind, it may be helpful if I clarify what I mean when I talk about *God's will.* I am referring to His purposes, plans, and desires, which can have both personal and worldwide implications. In other words, His will pertains to your life in a specific way, but it can also apply to how He is directing history, the nations, and all humanity.

For example, when the Lord promised Zacharias and Elizabeth that they would have a baby boy named John, He was speaking about His unique plans for that particular couple (Luke 1:5–25). But when God prophesied through Isaiah that we would be healed and our sins would be forgiven by the suffering of the Messiah (Isa. 53), He was speaking in a broader sense—not just the salvation of a particular person or nation, but of *anyone* who would believe in Christ's provision on the Cross (John 3:14–16).

Therefore, we should understand that God's will can range in scope from the minute details of your life to grand purposes which affect all creation. This is very important for you to remember as you wait, because the Father is actively working in both the overarching matters that concern you and in the particulars.

Likewise, we must realize that there are two major aspects to God's will. First, the Lord expresses a *determined will*, which is inevitable and unchangeable because it involves those plans He will absolutely accomplish. Nothing in all creation can impede Him from carrying them out because He is sovereign (Ps. 103:19). For example, in Chapter 2, we discussed how the Father bestowed the region of Canaan on Abraham's descendants and how He has faithfully restored the territory to them throughout history. Nothing can change the fact that Abraham's offspring will ultimately possess the Promised Land (Ezek. 47:13–14).

We also know that Jesus will return one day (Matt. 24:30), there will be a judgment (Heb. 9:27), and all whose names are written in the Lamb's Book of Life will be saved (Rev. 21:27). All of these promises are part of God's *determined will*, which cannot be inhibited. They will assuredly come to pass.

What this means for you as a believer is that you never have to worry about your salvation (Rom. 10:9–13) or your home in heaven (John 14:2–3). These are blessings that God has undeniably, resolutely provided for all who believe in Jesus. Likewise, you know that if the Lord calls you to embark on some special task or makes you an

unconditional promise—such as He did with David and Abraham—
He will enable you to accomplish it (Phil. 1:6).

But second, there is God's *desired will*, which includes His general
moral laws and His plans for each of us as individuals. Unlike His *determined* purposes, the Father's *desired* objectives may or may not be fulfilled because He allows us freedom in our daily choices. For example,
we know that the Lord's command is that hu-
manity avoid theft, lying, murder, or adultery   God's *desired*
because He said so in His Word (Ex. 20:13–16).   *will* includes His
But because people have the ability to make   general moral laws
decisions, these sins exist in the world.   and His plans

Likewise, we can resist what God wants   for each of us as
us to do in a *personal* sense. Throughout the   individuals.
years, I've met several people who were called
into the ministry, but instead of submitting to Him and experiencing
His wonderful plans for them, they fought the Lord and went their
own way. Sadly, every person I've known who refused to obey God's call
ultimately regretted it.

Therefore, what God's *desired will* means for you is that every day,
with each decision, you have a choice. You can seek the Lord and allow
Him to lead you, or you can resist Him. You can abide by His moral
laws and relate to others in the manner He instructs you to—with love,
joy, peace, patience, kindness, gentleness, self-control, and faithfulness
(Gal. 5:22–23). Or you can go the other way, choosing sexual immorality, divisiveness, fighting, jealousy, gossip, addiction, and selfish ambition
as your way of life (Gal. 5:19–21). You can look to Him for your purpose
or you can look to someone or something else to be your identity. You
make the decision whether or not to follow Him.

However, as I said before, God will move heaven and earth to show
you His will. This means if you are truly seeking Him, you cannot *miss*
His direction—which is what many believers fear. It is not hidden from
you. The Father wants to lead you, which is why He has placed His
Holy Spirit within you to direct you.

This is what the apostle Paul meant when he wrote Philippians 2:12–13, "Work out your salvation with fear and trembling; for it is God who is at work in you, both to will and to work for His good pleasure." This doesn't mean you have to do something to deserve or hold on to your salvation. Rather, Paul is assuring you of the Lord's direction and admonishes you to be sensitive and reverent about the way He is guiding you.

In his wonderful book, *My Utmost for His Highest*, Oswald Chambers explains it like this:

> Look to Jesus and you will find that your will and your conscience are in agreement with Him every time. What causes you to say "I will not obey" is something less deep and penetrating than your will. It is perversity or stubbornness, and they are never in agreement with God. . . . In someone who has been born again, the source of the will is Almighty God. " . . . for it is God who works in you both to will and to do for His good pleasure." With focused attention and great care, you have to "work out" what God "works in" you—not *work* to accomplish or earn "your own salvation," but *work it out* so you will exhibit the evidence of a life based with determined, unshakable faith on the complete and perfect redemption of the Lord. As you do this, you do not bring an opposing will up against God's will—God's will *is* your will. Your natural choices will be in accordance with God's will, and living this life will be as natural as breathing. Stubbornness is an unintelligent barrier, refusing enlightenment and blocking its flow. The only thing to do with this barrier of stubbornness is to blow it up with "dynamite," and the "dynamite" is obedience to the Holy Spirit. Do I believe that Almighty God is the Source of my will? God not only expects me to do His will, but He is in me to do it.

In other words, you have exactly what you need in order to know and do the Lord's will: the Holy Spirit who lives and works within you. He is always revealing the areas that must be "worked out" in order to be more like Christ. Likewise, He constantly gives you opportunities to walk in His wonderful purposes for your life and is faithful to adjust your path when you begin to drift. Therefore, you do not have to struggle to know God's will, and you do not have to manipulate your circumstances to make His plan happen. Rather, your energy should be employed in exhibiting faith and walking step-by-step with Him as time passes, because you know He is actively working in the unseen. And you can be certain that when your heart is inclined toward Him, He uses all the resources at His disposal to accomplish what concerns you (Ps. 103:19).

> You do not have to struggle to know God's will, and you do not have to manipulate your circumstances to make His plan happen.

Sadly, the opposite is true as well. You can miss His path for you *by choice* when you don't seek Him, when you act in a manner that contradicts His Word, when you decline to obey His call to you, and when you refuse to relinquish control of your situation. I have said before that you will never lose when you follow the Father. But understand this fact for certain: *You can never really win—not in a lasting, meaningful way—without Him.* If you walk away from the Father out of stubbornness or unbelief, you abandon the only One who understands the deepest needs of your heart and how to meet them.

But perhaps you're wondering, *What if I mess up? What if I've lived outside of God's will until now? Does that mean it's all over for me?* Friend, don't be discouraged if you've made poor decisions throughout your life. You don't have to figure out how to make up for your failings, and you don't have to be afraid that your life is over. The truth is, you can start over fresh because of the Father's loving grace and mercy, which are new every morning (Lam. 3:22–23). He knew before the beginning of time how you would make mistakes and wrong choices. In His sovereignty, He is able to work everything—even your missteps—for your ultimate good (Rom. 8:28).

You see, we tend to look at God's will as His all-encompassing plan for our lives—one big blueprint of where we should go and what we should do. But it is so much more than that. The Lord's desires for you include helping you reach your full potential and fulfilling the reasons He formed you as He did. Ephesians 2:10 says, "We are His workmanship, created in Christ Jesus for good works, which God prepared beforehand so that we would walk in them."

This means He recognizes all of your talents, skills, and abilities—even the innate ones, hidden in the fiber of your being and yet undiscovered. He knows the profound needs you have to feel a sense of belonging, worthiness, and competency, and He understands exactly what it would take to satisfy them. He also comprehends your failings, history, and fears more deeply than you do. So a very deep and meaningful part of His plan is to work through every bit of who you are, to bring out the very best of who you were created to be, and to glorify Himself through you—giving you a sustaining, rewarding, and eternal sense of significance.

PURSUING GOD'S WILL

Hopefully, by now you can see the wonderful purpose that can motivate you as you endure expectantly. While you wait, you *pursue the Lord's plan*—allowing Him to guide you decision by decision, and thereby deepening your relationship with Him as He prepares you for His answer. And in the process, He develops your character and brings out your finest qualities. His wonderful will can give you the hope you need each day to keep going, even when life is difficult, because you realize that He is working in every detail of your life for your ultimate benefit.

But how do you do so? How do you seek His guidance, know Him better, and become who He created you to be?

1. THROUGH GOD'S WORD

Because God wants you to know and do His will, you can be assured that He will make it known to you in His time and according to His plan. However, the main way He reveals His purposes for you is always through Scripture, which is His comprehensive instruction book for living. Psalm 119:105 proclaims, "Your word is a lamp to my feet and a light to my path"—and for good reason. Meditating on God's Word is absolutely essential for receiving His counsel and illuminating the way you should go.

In fact, one of the most valuable things I have ever inherited was my grandfather's well-worn Bible. It is the only copy of Scripture he ever used and its edges are completely tattered from his long hours of studying. As I told you in Chapter 1, my grandfather, George Washington Stanley, was a godly preacher and evangelist who taught me to love God's Word. I only visited him in Siler City, North Carolina, two or three times, but it was enough to set the course of my life. I was like a dry sponge that soaked up everything he said. But what interested me most about him was that he knew how to listen to the Father and seek out His will.

My time with Granddad created this desire deep within to hear from the Lord myself. So I began to meditate on Scripture the way he taught me. That is, I wouldn't just read the Bible—I would ask questions. "Lord God, what are You saying to me? How do You want me to apply this to my life? What is it I'm supposed to learn, Father?"

"Lord God, what are You saying to me? How do You want me to apply this to my life? What is it I'm supposed to learn, Father?"

This has helped me immeasurably throughout my life—especially in times of waiting. This is because the Holy Spirit supernaturally uses Scripture to lead us, train us, correct our erroneous thinking, convict us of sin, influence our decisions, or stop us when we are drifting from God's will for our lives (2 Tim. 3:16–17). Psalm 119:130 explains, "The unfolding of Your words gives light; it gives understanding to the simple." He helps us to see the reality of our circumstances and how to handle them in a manner that honors Him. He also calls upon the

Scripture we've hidden in our hearts to confirm His purposes for us (Ps. 119:11).

For example, a dear, godly couple I know searched for the right residence for ten years, but nowhere they looked seemed quite right. One day, however, they were looking over a particularly beautiful parcel of land, and the Father spoke to the husband's heart by reminding him of Deuteronomy 11:24 (KJV), "Every place whereon the soles of your feet shall tread shall be yours." This, of course, was the promise the Lord gave to the children of Israel as they entered the land of Canaan. This verse impressed the man so profoundly that the couple decided to walk around the entire property. As they did, they saw all the wonderful ways the Father was providing the specific details they had prayed for throughout the years—above and beyond all they had asked or imagined. And they immediately knew that God was confirming this was the place they would call home.

The Lord can affirm His plan for you through Scripture as well. Psalm 16:11 promises, "You will make known to me the path of life; in Your presence is fullness of joy; in Your right hand there are pleasures forever." Therefore, as you open the Word of God, say to Him, "Father, I want to know You better. Speak to me, Lord. How do You want me to apply this to my life? What is it I'm supposed to learn? Show me the truth about Yourself and teach me the way I should go." You can be certain that this is a request He is always happy to fulfill.

2. THROUGH PRAYER

Inseparably linked with reading Scripture is seeking the Lord through prayer. After all, if you want to know what God's will is, doesn't it make sense to ask Him, "Lord, what would You have me do in this matter? What direction do You want me to take?" Of course it does. However, this also means that when you pray, you don't just keep talking. Rather, you spend time *listening* to what the Father is saying to you. You shut out the distractions and pay attention to what the Lord is communicating.

I learned to do this early in life. Of course, my mind used to drift just like anyone else's would. And when I was a boy, we didn't live in a large house, so I had to seek out a place in my church to pray. But I delivered newspapers early in the day, so when I was done, I would go down into the church's basement area, go through three different doors, and shut myself in the quietest, most remote Sunday School classroom I could find. I loved it because I could pray all I wanted to—as loudly and for however long I needed to.

In time, however, I realized that one of the best things about that little room was the fact that—being in the basement—it had no windows. When I went in there and shut the door, it was dark and absolutely silent, which totally eliminated any distractions. It was just God and me. So as Scripture, concerns, circumstances, or emotions came to mind, I would ask Him about them. "Father, why am I thinking about this right now? Is there something else I need to pray about for this problem? What do you want me to do about my concern?"

You see, when you and I pray, we are not alone—and God is not just taking our list of requests. Rather, the Lord is actively communicating what He desires for us. How does He do so? Jesus explained, "The Helper, the Holy Spirit . . . He will teach you all things, and bring to your remembrance all that I said to you" (John 14:26). In other words, the Spirit conveys His direction to us. Of course, it's not just His will about the desires of our hearts or problems we face that He's addressing, but He is also aligning us with His will. Inch-by-inch, step-by-step, thought-by-thought, and issue-by-issue, He is breaking strongholds, preparing us for what is ahead, and steering us on the right path.

That is the awesome promise of our wonderful holy, wise, omnipotent God. We may not know what wound the Father wants to heal or how He is leading us, but we don't have to. Why? Because, "The Spirit also helps our weakness; for we do not know how to pray as we should, but the Spirit Himself intercedes for us with groanings too deep for words; and He who searches the hearts knows what the mind of the Spirit is, because He intercedes for the saints according to the will of

God" (Rom. 8:26–27). He guides us to deal with what is necessary in accordance with the Father's plans for us.

Now, in the beginning of this chapter, we talked about 1 John 5:14–15, which is one of my anchor verses when it comes to prayer. "This is the confidence which we have before Him, that, if we ask anything according to His will, He hears us. And if we know that He hears us in whatever we ask, we know that we have the requests which we have asked from Him." Friend, you can know beyond a shadow of a doubt that if you are asking God for direction and are truly willing to listen to and obey Him, then you are praying "according to His will."

> If you're asking for something that would ultimately hurt you or doesn't fit His design for your life, the Lord will change your heart.

And as we just discussed, the Holy Spirit will show you what you should address and whether or not the desires you're praying about are His plan for you. If you're asking for something that would ultimately hurt you or doesn't fit His design for your life, the Lord will change your heart. It may take time, but your heavenly Father wants the best for you. So don't worry about whether you're making the right request. Instead, kneel before the throne of grace in reverence to Him, be observant of His promptings, and rely on Him to direct you to His wonderful blessings.

3. THROUGH CIRCUMSTANCES

Another way we understand God's will is through the circumstances of our lives. Keep this important principle foremost in your heart: the Lord is with each one of His children every single moment of the day. He promises, "I will never desert you, nor will I ever forsake you" (Heb. 13:5). That means God is not just with us in the emergencies, which is when many people wait to call upon Him. Rather, He is living within us every second and is guiding the circumstances of our lives.

If you recall, Romans 8:28 says, "God causes *all things* to work together for good to those who love God, to those who are called according to His purpose" (emphasis added). How many of the events of our lives does the Father employ for our benefit? Every one of them. And so, if He is arranging all details for our advantage—and He is— then moment-by-moment He must be involved in them.

For example, say a fellow is looking for a job and he submits applications for three positions that on the surface look comparable—the requirements, salary, benefits, and advancement opportunities are all similar. So he prays, "Lord, I'm available and I desire to do Your will. Whatever You want is what I will do. Please show me which job is the one You desire for me." He goes to the interviews, which all go well, but after a few days, he discovers the first of the positions has been given to another person.

As time goes on, however, he receives offers from the other two employers and wonders which one to choose. He runs into a friend who he hasn't seen in a while, and he shares about his job search. The friend knows some of the background of the second company he applied to— and it is not good. As the friend is speaking, the man recalls that during his interview he felt as if something was not right with that particular situation—there was some hesitancy in his spirit about that second company. So he goes home and prays. As he is talking to the Father, he realizes that he has a perfect peace in his heart about letting that second opportunity go and taking hold of the third and final job offer.

Doors being opened or closed, the timely acquisition of information, a restless spirit, a peace in the soul that transcends understanding—all of these are ways that the Father will work through your situation to direct you. So remember: *The circumstances of your life are extremely important.* From a well-timed sermon or devotion, to new acquaintances, to the instruction of those in authority over you, to even the most unusual occurrences—like Moses seeing the burning bush (Ex. 3)—God can use all of it to speak to you. Nothing touches you without Him allowing it.

Now, please notice: I did *not* say the Lord *causes* all the conditions or problems that affect you. Sometimes the reason you'll experience trouble is because of the consequences of your own or another's actions. But God can work through everything that happens to position you for greater blessing and to glorify Himself. And if you will pay attention to what the Father is doing through your circumstances, you will learn a great deal about His will for your life.

For example, suppose you are in the midst of a situation that makes you exceedingly irate. For some reason, whenever you think about it, your blood pressure begins to rise and you become so frustrated and overwrought that you don't know what to do with yourself. Instead of getting even madder every time you consider it, stop and ask, "Lord God, why did You allow this in my life? I know this anger is a warning flag. What is it You want me to see in this situation?" It could be that you need to forgive someone; that you have some unacknowledged jealousy, pride, or fear in your heart; or that there are deep areas of hurt within you that the Father wants to heal. Perhaps you are too attached to the situation, and the Lord is separating you from it. It could also be that what you feel is righteous indignation and that God wants you to take a stand for the sake of His name.

Whatever it is, if you will turn your attention to what the Father is teaching you through it, you will take important steps on the path of His will. But if you ignore or refuse to deal with it, you may be delaying His answer to your prayers even further.

4. THROUGH GODLY COUNSEL

The final way God will reveal His will to us is through the wise counsel of others. We see how important this is throughout Proverbs:

- "A wise man will hear and increase in learning, and a man of understanding will acquire wise counsel" (1:5).
- "Where there is no guidance the people fall, but in abundance of counselors there is victory" (11:4).
- "The way of a fool is right in his own eyes, but a wise man is he who listens to counsel" (12:15).
- "Through insolence comes nothing but strife, but wisdom is with those who receive counsel" (13:10).
- "Without consultation, plans are frustrated, but with many counselors they succeed" (15:22).
- "Listen to counsel and accept discipline, that you may be wise the rest of your days" (19:20).
- "By wise guidance you will wage war, and in abundance of counselors there is victory" (24:6).

With this in mind, I would ask, *Do you have a friend or loved one that you can go to for godly counsel, who you know will be wise and discreet in the guidance he or she gives you?* I am not talking about anyone who will simply give you advice or who would tell you what he or she would do in your situation. That's not helpful at all. Everyone will have an opinion about what course you should take, and they will usually point you in the wrong direction.

Rather, I am talking about someone who is obviously submitted to the Father and obeying Him—a Christian who clearly understands how to listen to God and has a strong relationship with Him. Friend, it is crucial that before you take any recommendations from another believer, you look at his or her life and ask "Is this individual living in God's will?" The last person you want to get counsel from is somebody who is actively disobeying the Father. You want someone with whom it is very evident that he or she is walking in the center of His path for them.

Likewise, never ask, "Would you please tell me God's will for my life?" or, "What should I do?" Those are not the right questions. Instead, inquire, "On the basis of your relationship with the Lord and your knowledge of His Word, do you have any insight into how God may be leading me? What does Scripture say about my situation?" A good friend will have your spiritual growth and well-being in mind as he or she advises you and will keep your conversations confidential for your protection. A godly counselor will

"What does Scripture say about my situation?"

be motivated to guide you to the truth—even when it is uncomfortable or it hurts—because he or she will want to see you break free from bondage and follow Christ in obedience. Ultimately, this person's desire will be for you to have a strong relationship with the Father so you can experience life at its best. That is the kind of friend whose counsel you can trust.

For example, when my children were growing up, they would come to me with different questions, and I would tell them, "You just need to ask God about that."

I can still remember how they would say, "Oh, Dad! Can't you just tell us? We don't know Him like you do. Suppose we make a mistake." Of course, it would have been easier for me just to tell them what to do and not risk them going off on the wrong path. That's what most people desire—they just want someone to direct them rather than struggling to understand the Lord's will on their own. But I realized that these were wonderful opportunities for Andy and Becky to grow in their relationships with Jesus. If I had just revealed the wise course of action to them, it wouldn't help them one bit.

So I would respond, "The only way you'll learn how to find God's will is to start by asking Him now. Don't worry; I'll help you. But you have to make the effort to find out."

Well, on one occasion, they were asking me about something they wanted to do and I realized they were testing their boundaries. So, as usual, I asked them, "What does God say about it?"

They replied, "He said it was all right."

Well, I knew it wasn't, so I said, "Let's get the Bible and find out." And I led them to some Scripture passages to consider. Eventually, they made the right choice.

But I write all this to show you that a godly counselor will not be interested in imposing his or her own view or demanding you do as he or she says. Rather, that individual will be concerned with helping you discover the biblical principles that will grow your relationship with Christ. Remember, the question isn't, "What do you think I ought to do?" It is, "What does God's Word say about my situation?" No one can tell you the Father's will for your life, but a godly friend can walk with you, encourage you, and help you stay on track as you seek Him.

CONFIRMING GOD'S WILL

Of course, I realize that as you're reading this, you may be thinking, *This is all well and good, Dr. Stanley. But I want to know God's will about my heart's desire. Is He leading me to it or isn't He?*

To that I would say, "Friend, do you trust the Lord to guide you in the highest and noblest way possible?" I hope you would answer, "Yes." And I pray you realize that though He may not show you what your destination is, and though the desires and goals God has put on your heart may appear very far away, indeed, your heavenly Father is leading you step-by-step with love, wisdom, and power to His very best for your life. He may not show you the whole picture all at once. But be assured, He would not withhold any blessing that is truly good for you (Ps. 84:11).

With this in mind, realize that your godly dreams may be an important part of your Christian walk that the Lord uses to inspire you and fulfill the plans He has for you (Ps. 37:4–5). God-given desires can motivate you to press on even through terrible adversity. So evaluate the hopes that drive you: Do they align with the Lord's plans for you? Do they encourage you to grow closer to Him? Or are they working against His purposes for your life?

So that you can figure out the answers to these important questions, here is a seven-fold test that will help you ascertain whether or not a particular path, decision, or dream is the Father's will for your life. As you ask yourself these questions, the Holy Spirit will bear witness to your spirit whether you are headed in the right direction or the wrong one.

1. *Is this choice consistent with the Word of God?* The Lord will never tell you to do anything that contradicts Scripture, so you can be confident in looking to the Bible for direction. For example, as we discussed previously, you can know for certain that it is never God's will for you to lie, steal from others, commit murder, or have an adulterous affair, because He states it clearly in His Word (Ex. 20:13–16). Likewise, you know that, "The fruit of the Spirit is love, joy, peace, patience, kindness, goodness, faithfulness, gentleness, self-control; against such things there is no law" (Gal. 5:22–23). So when you act out of your God-given love, joy, peace, etc., you know you are acting in a godly manner. However, never attempt to take a passage out of context to justify your stance. For example, you cannot say you are being compassionate by stealing from one person and giving to another. Biblical principles remain consistent throughout the whole counsel of Scripture—you cannot violate one command to fulfill another. In the next chapter, we'll look at how to know whether or not the verses you're reading apply to your situation and are a promise God has given for you to hold on to.

2. *Is this a wise decision?* How will this choice shape your future? Will you face consequences because of it? For example, it may seem like a good idea to spend a great deal of money on something you want right now. But how will being in deep debt affect you tomorrow and the next day? Will satisfying that desire today mean sacrificing important

goals in the days, weeks, and years to come? Remember, "The fear of the LORD is the beginning of wisdom, and the knowledge of the Holy One is understanding" (Prov. 9:10). Are you making your decisions with God in mind?

3. *Can you honestly ask God to enable you to achieve this goal?* Does what you are seeking fit His character? Is it appropriate for you as someone who represents Him in the world? Throughout my life, I've seen plenty of people who wanted the Father to bless their dishonest and ungodly schemes, but He absolutely will not do it. Galatians 6:7–8 is clear, "Do not be deceived, God is not mocked; for whatever a man sows, this he will also reap. For the one who sows to his own flesh will from the flesh reap corruption, but the one who sows to the Spirit will from the Spirit reap eternal life." The Lord is not going to cater to wicked, fleshly desires—no matter what they may be or why you may have them. Rather, He wants you to be conformed to the image of Jesus (Rom. 8:29). Therefore, if you're tempted to ask the Lord for something that you know is contrary to His character, you can be sure it's not His will for you and that you must not pursue it.

> If you're tempted to ask the Lord for something that you know is contrary to His character, you can be sure it's not His will for you and that you must not pursue it.

4. *Do you have genuine peace about this path?* Remember, harmony with God is the fruit of oneness with Him. In fact, in Greek, the word "peace," *eirene*, means, "to bind together." Jesus joins us to Himself, bringing us into unity and agreement with the Father about His plan for our lives. So when we are about to make a decision that is in His will, we will certainly feel a sense of tranquility (Col. 3:15). Of course, you can manufacture a false outward calm by convincing yourself that everything is fantastic.

But the proof is in your time with God. Do you experience peace in His presence? If your choices are causing you to feel restless when you pray or if you're motivated to avoid Him altogether, you can be certain that the path you're asking about is not in line with His plans for you.

5. *Is this decision appropriate for who you are as a follower of Jesus?* In other words, would you recommend this choice to another Christian? If other believers knew about your conduct, would they approve? You inherently know that certain behaviors are not appropriate for you as a redeemed child of the living God. In fact, you most likely hide those actions from others because you feel some embarrassment whenever you engage in them and you know that they would tarnish your testimony. Friend, shame and humiliation are never God's will for you. If there are activities in your life that harm you or cause you to feel dishonor, confess them to your heavenly Father, repent of them, and allow Him to lead you to freedom.

6. *Does this fit God's overall plan for your life?* Now, let me be absolutely clear: The Lord has a great purpose for you. It may not seem that way to you right now. Depending on how you were raised, you may feel as if your life has no genuine meaning or significance. But know this for certain—the Father has designed you with His excellent reasons in mind, and He has wonderful goals He desires to accomplish through your life. Psalm 139:13–16 declares,

> You formed my inward parts;
> You wove me in my mother's womb.
> I will give thanks to You, for I am fearfully and wonderfully made;
> Wonderful are Your works,
> And my soul knows it very well.
> My frame was not hidden from You,

When I was made in secret,
And skillfully wrought in the depths of the earth;
Your eyes have seen my unformed substance;
And in Your book were all written
The days that were ordained for me,
When as yet there was not one of them.

In other words, the Father did not just react to your birth.
He formed you; designed your features; and had a plan for
your life, your potential, and all you could accomplish even
before you existed. There has never been nor will there ever
be another person like you. He loves you unconditionally,
sincerely, and uniquely—as if you were the only person on
earth. In light of this, then, it is important for you to consider
whether your choices support or oppose His path for your
life. As we've discussed, if you choose to stray from His plan,
you will ultimately be abandoning the only One who can
lead you to true joy and fulfillment.

7. *Will this decision honor God?* Are you demonstrating your respect and reverence for the Father by doing this? Is it evident
   by your actions that He is the Lord of your life? Or does this
   decision indicate that you are really relying on and serving
   something or someone else? As we discussed in Chapter 3,
   the Lord will not tolerate anything to come before Him in
   your priorities. So if you are satisfying an idol, the Father
   will reveal it to you.

Friend, consider these questions very carefully and prayerfully, and
in time, God will make it crystal clear whether your heart's desire is
His will for your life. He longs to give you abundant blessings and the
fullness of joy. So as He reveals His path to you, allow your dreams to
be conformed to His will, and follow His guidance faithfully. If you do,

I promise that you will experience His very best blessings and your life will be filled with His awesome purpose.

———————————————◆———————————————

Father, how grateful I am that You are so ready to reveal Your wonderful plan for my life. I want to obey You, Lord. I want to know Your will and fulfill the good goals You've set before me. Thank You for loving me so much and for giving my life purpose.

Lord, it is difficult, but I also praise You for this time of waiting and how it is motivating me to seek You. I realize that during this time You are revealing Your ways to me, helping me to know You better, conforming me to Your wonderful character, and disciplining me so I can reach my full potential. Thank You, Father. Please make knowing You and pursuing Your will the reason I get out of bed every morning and the focus of my life. With this in mind, I ask that You would fill me with passion for Your Word, a longing to tarry with You in prayer, discernment of Your purpose in every circumstance, and wisdom in choosing godly counselors.

And Father, please show me whether or not this dear desire of my heart is in keeping with Your plans for my life. Lord, if there is any way it dishonors You, violates Your Word, demonstrates a lack of wisdom, or doesn't fit who You are forming me to be, please reveal it to me and change my heart. But Lord, if this yearning is Your will for me, then show me that as well by giving me Your peace that transcends understanding and guiding me to promises to hold on to in Scripture.

Thank You for loving me, Lord. And thank You for leading me to the best life has to offer. In Your holy name I pray, beloved Jesus. Amen.

———————————————◆———————————————

POINTS FOR ACTIVE WAITING

1. Memorize Philippians 2:13, "It is God who is at work in you, both to will and to work for His good pleasure."
2. Whenever you feel anxious because of this season of delay, repeat Philippians 2:13, Proverbs 3:5–6, Psalm 62:5–6, and Psalm 27:14 to yourself.
3. Are you seeking God's will? Today and every day, spend time reading Scripture. As the Father brings verses to your attention, ask Him, "Lord God, what are You saying to me? How do You want me to apply this to my life? What is it I'm supposed to learn?"
4. Likewise, spend time in prayer daily. As Bible passages, concerns, situations, or emotions come to mind, ask Him, "Father, why is this surfacing now? Is there something here I need to deal with? How would You have me proceed?"
5. As God leads you to a course of action, review the seven ways you can confirm His will (beginning on page 120). Continue to evaluate your motives and decisions each day and be sure to conform your desires to His will as He reveals it to you.
6. Remember to thank God daily for leading you on His wonderful path for your life and for faithfully accomplishing all that concerns you (Ps. 57:2).

Use this space to respond to the "Points for Active Waiting" and to record prayer requests, key lessons God is teaching you, and your insights about waiting on the Lord to act on your behalf.

Let us hold fast the confession
of our hope without wavering,
for He who promised is faithful.
—Hebrews 10:23

5

CLAIMING GOD'S PROMISES

Actively Expressing Faith in the Delays

There is an important principle in Scripture that once you learn and apply it, will open the door to the treasure houses of heaven for you. You especially need this principle during times of waiting because it will keep you steady and strong as the storms of adversity and waves of doubt arise. What is this crucial precept? It's the principle of *claiming* the Lord's promises to you.

In the last chapter, we discussed finding purpose during seasons of delay by pursuing God's will. And as you seek the Father's face by reading the Bible, no doubt certain passages will stand out to you as especially meaningful. So in this chapter we will look at how you can know for certain that a biblical assurance is for you. And we'll talk about how claiming God's promises help you persevere with hope as you wait for Him.

To understand the dynamic, positive effect God's promises can have on our times of waiting, let's recall the definition from Chapter 1: Waiting signifies an expectant endurance that is demonstrated by a *directed*, *purposeful*, *active*, and *courageous* attitude of prayer. The third characteristic in that definition is that we must be *active*.

Many people may believe waiting is passive, but that is not what the Lord intended for us as believers. Yes, we are *still* in the sense that we take our hands off our situation and allow the Father to work through our circumstances. But we are also to be *active* in growing spiritually—and we do so by resolutely taking hold of His Word. As we discover God's will, we actively claim His promises and continue obeying Him step-by-step.

Think of it like this: just as we work on our physical muscles in a gym, this time of waiting is an opportunity to develop our spiritual muscles—our faith, hope, and perseverance. We do so by making the deliberate decision to incorporate Scripture into our lives and to have faith the Father is working on our behalf. We eagerly take hold of the promises He's given us in the Bible, vigorously set our hearts to believe Him, and energetically obey whenever He calls. And as we make the active choice to trust His promises, our hope grows and we learn to face the time of delay with expectant endurance.

Thankfully, because the Sovereign God of the universe has never faltered in fulfilling His word, we are absolutely assured He will not fail us now. Our active resolve to trust Him will certainly lead to blessing.

With this in mind, Hebrews 10:35–36 admonishes, "Do not throw away your confidence, which has a great reward. For you have need of endurance, so that when you have done the will of God, you may receive what was promised." The Living Bible paraphrases it like this, "Do not let this happy trust in the Lord die away, no matter what happens. Remember your reward! You need to keep on patiently doing God's will if you want him to do for you all that he has promised."

> The Sovereign God of the universe has never faltered in fulfilling His word and He will not fail us now.

In other words, our perseverance is key for receiving the very best God has planned for us. Therefore, we must endure—walking in His will no matter what happens or how long it takes so we can know for certain that we will receive the blessings He has planned for us. And we do so by actively clinging to Him and claiming what He's promised us.

As I said, understanding this will open the door to the treasure houses of heaven for you and will help you face your times of waiting victoriously.

GOD'S WONDERFUL ASSURANCES

Although I do not have any idea how many promises are in the Bible—I've been too busy claiming them to stop and count them—this much I do know: God has an answer for every need you or I could ever experience. So let us begin by defining what these assurances are and what they can mean to each of us.

A biblical promise is a declaration of God's intention to graciously bestow a gift upon a person or group of people. That is, the Lord makes a commitment that He will perform a particular act or give a certain blessing.

Likewise, the apostle Peter teaches us that the guarantees the Father makes to us throughout Scripture are both "precious and magnificent" (2 Pet. 1:4). The Greek word for "precious," *timios*, means, "of exceedingly great value, costly, honored, highly esteemed, or especially dear." Likewise, the term for "magnificent," *megistos*, signifies they are "preeminent, greatest, and strongest." Therefore, not only do we know that God's promises are His wonderful gifts to us, but they are extremely valuable and more astounding than we can imagine. The assurances that our loving heavenly Father gives us exceed the highest honor and worth our imaginations can conceive.

> A biblical promise is a declaration of God's intention to graciously bestow a gift upon a person or group of people.

Undoubtedly we can see that this is true in the promise of John 3:16, "God so loved the world, that He gave His only begotten Son, that whoever believes in Him shall not perish, but have eternal life." The thought that the almighty, omniscient, sovereign Lord of all creation loved us so deeply as His children that He would reach down and make it possible for us to live with Him in heaven forever—well, that is certainly more wonderful than the mind can comprehend. The entirety of our eternal life is wrapped up in that simple, splendid promise.

So this is what I would have you see here: As you wait on God, He gives you assurances of His blessings for you that are "far more than [you] would ever dare to ask or even dream of—infinitely beyond [your] highest prayers, desires, thoughts, or hopes" (Eph. 3:20, TLB). And as you actively claim them, they help you endure the delays.

THE SOURCE OF THE PROMISE

Now you and I both realize that a promise is only as strong and as sure as the character of the one making it. Most likely, you've had people in your life, like I have, who were not trustworthy or reliable. Their failure to carry through on their oaths—whether deliberately or for reasons beyond their control—affected us deeply and may even have made us somewhat cynical. And when the ones breaking their pledges are loved ones or people in authority, the effect can be especially damaging.

It can become difficult for us to trust, especially as the days and weeks wear on. We appreciate the fact that the Lord gives these astounding promises to us, but can we really be sure He will fulfill them? If people we can see, hear, and touch have let us down, why wouldn't He?

Thankfully, throughout Scripture we are assured of God's faithfulness to keep His word.

- "Not one of the good promises which the Lord had made to the house of Israel failed; all came to pass" (Josh. 21:45).
- "Not one word of all the good words which the Lord your God spoke concerning you has failed; all have been fulfilled for you, not one of them has failed" (Josh. 23:14).
- "The Lord has fulfilled His word which He spoke" (1 Kings 8:20).
- "Not one word has failed of all His good promise" (1 Kings 8:56).

- "You have promised him; indeed You have spoken with Your mouth and have fulfilled it with Your hand" (2 Chron. 6:15).
- "You have fulfilled Your promise, for You are righteous" (Neh. 9:8).
- "All this took place to fulfill what was spoken by the Lord" (Matt. 1:22).
- "Let us hold fast the confession of our hope without wavering, for He who promised is faithful" (Heb. 10:23).

All history testifies that the Father always keeps His promises. Likewise, we have seen throughout this book that the Lord miraculously accomplished all He told Abraham and David. Therefore, if God assures you of something in His Word, you can be confident that He will not fulfill just some of it, most of it, or ninety-nine percent of it. He will carry out His guarantee to you *completely*, beyond what you ask or expect.

In fact, the Lord declares, "So will My word be which goes forth from My mouth; it will not return to Me empty, without accomplishing what I desire, and without succeeding in the matter for which I sent it" (Isa. 55:11). He is not unreliable, capricious, or limited like others who have broken their promises to us—and it is always a mistake to think of Him as such. Rather, the Lord is faithful, abundantly more than able, and absolutely determined to achieve what concerns us. He delights in meeting the needs of His children. Therefore, we can always be positive that whatever assurances God gives us, He will be certain to bring them to fruition no matter what.

APPROPRIATING PROMISES:
LIMITED VERSUS GENERAL

So how can you and I be sure that a particular promise is for us? And once we identify a passage in Scripture that is meaningful to us, how can we appropriate it and claim it for our own?

First, we must understand that not every promise of Scripture is intended for us. In fact, there are many blessings God has pledged throughout His Word that are meant for specific people and nations.

For example, we observed how the Lord uniquely anointed David to be the future king of Israel in 1 Samuel 16:13. Is this a verse anyone can claim? Can anyone rule the people of Israel? Of course not. It was decidedly intended for David in that particular time in Israel's history.

Therefore, the way I assess these biblical assurances is to categorize them as either *general* or *limited*. *General promises* are available for any believer who desires to claim them. For example, Jesus says, "Ask, and it will be given to you; seek, and you will find; knock, and it will be opened to you. For everyone who asks receives, and he who seeks finds, and to him who knocks it will be opened." We know we can appropriate that promise with confidence because Jesus Himself said we could.

> *General promises are available for any believer who desires to claim them.*

Limited promises, however, are given to a specific person, group, or nation, usually during an identifiable time, for a distinctive purpose that God desires to carry out. For example, in the previous chapter we talked about how the Lord prophesied through Isaiah that our sins would be forgiven by the suffering of the Messiah. So as we read the promise, "The Righteous One, My Servant, will justify the many, as He will bear their iniquities" (53:11), we realize that this assurance is limited—not just anyone can bear the transgressions of the world or provide salvation. Only our sinless, sacrificial, substitutionary Savior Jesus could do so and make us acceptable before the Father.

Additionally, we saw in Genesis 18:10 that God told Abraham, "I will surely return to you at this time next year; and behold, Sarah your wife will have a son." Then the Lord spoke again in verse fourteen and affirmed, "Is anything too difficult for the LORD? At the appointed time I will return to you, at this time next year, and Sarah will have a son."

Was this an assurance for anyone who desires to have a baby? No. This promise was expressly given to Abraham and Sarah and was *limited* in its application. And we know that God had a very specific goal in mind when He gave Isaac to this faithful couple, which was to eventually establish the twelve tribes of Israel and the lineage of Jesus the Messiah. So this is not an assurance that *anyone* can claim as their own. You cannot just choose this passage of Scripture as a promise God will fulfill for you.

However, there is an exception. It could be that as you are reading these verses, the Spirit of God speaks to your heart in a strong and unmistakable way, "I'm going to give you a child as I did for Sarah." There is a tremendous difference between the Lord announcing what He will do in your life and you simply finding this verse and appropriating it as a promise.

This is why it is absolutely essential that you learn how to listen to the Father and discern when His Spirit is speaking to you. In these cases, you know for certain that it's not just your imagination interpreting your circumstances in a manner that caters to your desires. Rather, you have *discernment*—you understand when the Spirit of God is speaking to you, revealing a biblical principle you can live by, and making known His plans for your life.

I can remember many times when this has happened to me—when the Lord proclaimed what He was going to do in my life. One that sticks out in my mind was when I was dealing with a situation that was very difficult, complicated, and potentially explosive. I didn't have any idea about how to manage a particular disagreement in the church, and it was getting completely out of control. So I cried out, "God, I need some real wisdom about this."

> It is absolutely essential that you learn how to listen to the Father and discern when His Spirit is speaking to you.

I prayed about it for weeks. Then one morning I was reading those beautiful verses in Isaiah 9 about how the coming Messiah would be our Wonderful Counselor and Prince of Peace (v. 6). Suddenly, a particular phrase in verse seven struck me, "The zeal of the Lord will accomplish it." Now, this passage is a *limited* promise about how God will establish the Messianic kingdom. However, the Holy Spirit spoke straight to my heart that He would handle the conflict—I would not have to do a thing about it. All that was required was that I quietly trust the Father and watch Him work. Of course, this directly corresponds with a principle I have spoken of often: God works on behalf of those who wait for Him. So I knew I could have confidence that this promise was for me. Sure enough, in just a few days, the Lord took care of the whole situation. I didn't have to do a thing.

Therefore, at certain times the Father can and will speak to us through these limited promises, even when they only apply to specific people, times, or situations. This is especially true when they illustrate overarching principles about how God meets the needs, grants the desires, and works in the lives of His children, as He did with me. Since His ways never change, we can count on Him to work in a similar manner in our lives (Heb. 13:8).

APPROPRIATING GENERAL PROMISES: CONDITIONAL VERSUS UNCONDITIONAL

So, to review, *general promises* are available for any believer who desires to claim them. *Limited promises* are given to a specific person, group, or nation, usually during an identifiable time, for a distinctive purpose that God desires to carry out.

Now, among the *general* assurances, there are two types of commitments the Lord will make to us as Christians, and they are *unconditional* and *conditional*.

An *unconditional promise* is a guarantee the Father gives us that has no exceptions or qualifications. In other words, there is nothing we must do in order to receive it. No matter what happens, God will fulfill it. For example, in John 14:2–3, Jesus assures believers, "In My Father's house are many dwelling places; if it were not so, I would have told you; for I go to prepare a place for you. If I go and prepare a place for you, I will come again and receive you to Myself, that where I am, there you may be also." This is an unqualified guarantee that our Savior makes to us as Christians—regardless of our fruit, once we accept Him as Savior, we will have a home in heaven.

A *conditional promise*, on the other hand, is subject to certain requirements. For example, in 1 John 1:9 we read, "If we confess our sins, He is faithful and righteous to forgive us our sins and to cleanse us from all unrighteousness." We can receive His pardon and purification if we will first repent. That is, His assurance to us is dependent upon our acknowledgment that we have sinned and our commitment to turn away from the destructive behavior.

In fact, as we look at all the promises in God's Word, the majority of them are conditional—most of them require us to obey the Father in one way or another. People often claim verses without obeying God's conditions and then wonder why the Lord does not answer them. Conditional promises have a responsibility attached to the assurance that must be observed. Look at these wonderful passages, which we so often cling to:

- "Cast your burden upon the Lord and He will sustain you" (Ps. 55:22). What is the condition? That we release our encumbrances to Him.
- "Trust in the LORD with all your heart and do not lean on your own understanding. In all your ways acknowledge Him, and He will make your paths straight" (Prov. 3:5–6). What is the requirement? That we have faith in Him and recognize His leadership in every situation.
- " 'I know the plans that I have for you,' declares the LORD, 'plans for welfare and not for calamity to give you a future and a hope. Then you will call upon Me and come and pray to Me, and I will listen to you. You will seek Me and find *Me* when you search for Me with all your heart' " (Jer. 29:11–13). What is the prerequisite for experiencing the awesome plans of God? We must call upon Him, pray to Him, and seek Him wholeheartedly.

Therefore, as you are reading God's Word and certain passages stand out to you, remember that it is crucial for you to ascertain whether they are limited or general, conditional or unconditional. This will help you understand whether the Father intended those verses for you and whether you are able to meet the requirements associated with them.

IS THIS PROMISE FOR ME?

Of course, what most people are interested in is whether or not a biblical assurance applies to their specific situation. And as you are waiting on God, you need a firm and steadfast anchor you can hold on to as the days, weeks, and months go by so you will not grow discouraged. Remember, we are discussing how you can endure the delays victoriously—with hope and perseverance. To do so, you must *actively* claim His word and continue obeying Him step-by-step. As Psalm 119:50 (NLT) says, "Your promise revives me; it comforts me in all my troubles." But in order for you to appropriate an assurance successfully, you must be certain that the Father meant it for you and the particular longing you are wrestling with.

So how can you know for sure? How can you take hold of a promise from God and be confident that it is really for you? Throughout the years, this is the criteria I have used to answer that very question.

First, does this promise meet a particular need or desire the Lord wants to fulfill?
For example, all of us require direction when it comes to our decisions, and as we have seen repeatedly, God is pleased to lead us. So in Psalm 32:8 He promises, "I will instruct you and teach you in the way which you should go; I will counsel you with My eye upon you." The Father specifically commits to meeting this need. He *will* guide you.

Likewise, you can know for certain that if you "hunger and thirst for righteousness," you will be filled (Matt. 5:6). If you desire to be "conformed to the image of His Son," the Father will empower you in that pursuit (Rom. 8:29). Throughout Scripture, the Lord enumerates many necessities He is glad to provide for. In fact, at the end of this chapter, you will find a list of some of the wonderful ways the Lord answers your deepest needs. So review those promises, ask the Father for guidance, search God's Word, and consider carefully whether or not your request is one He delights to fulfill.

> Throughout Scripture, the Lord enumerates many necessities He is glad to provide for.

Second, does the context of the Scripture allow it?
As we've been discussing, you cannot merely choose a promise from the Bible without regard to its background and intent. Therefore, whenever you find a passage that is exceptionally meaningful to you, consider to whom it was originally directed, whether or not a wider application of it is appropriate, and if there are requirements that must accompany its fulfillment.

Third, does the fulfillment of this promise glorify Him?
Of course, the Lord makes these commitments to us because He loves us unconditionally and wants to give us guidance, provision, and protection. But He also does so to reveal His awesome wisdom, power, and grace. We need to keep this in mind because His fulfilled promises are part of our testimony—one of the ways He makes Himself known to those around us. Therefore, if a request would ultimately harm you or be hurtful to another person, does not honor Him or fit His character, or could stop someone else from seeking Him, it is most likely not in His plan for you.

Fourth, is this promise consistent with His will for your life?
In the previous chapter, we discussed the importance of walking in the center of God's path for you, knowing Him better, and becoming all He

created you to be. The assurances He gives you, therefore, will generally support what He is calling you to accomplish. For example, if the Father is calling you into full-time ministry, you can count on Him to enable you to serve Him (1 Pet. 4:11). As I have often said, God assumes full responsibility for your needs when you obey Him.

However, if what you ask Him opposes His will for you—even if it is simply that His timing and methods don't match your hopes or expectations—His purposes for you will take precedence. When this happens, it is crucial for you to remember that He has something much better in mind for you. Therefore, as you pray, be sure to ask God if the promise you desire to claim is rightfully aligned with His plans for your life.

Fifth, are you walking in obedience to Him?

Are you submitting to God and carrying out what He wants you to do as best you know how? Doing so gives you the right and privilege to claim His promises. But as we saw in Chapter 3, if you are rebellious and living according to your own desires, you will forfeit your ability to take hold of His wonderful assurances. Isaiah 59:1–2 explains, "The LORD's hand is not so short that it cannot save; nor is His ear so dull that it cannot hear. But your iniquities have made a separation between you and your God, and your sins have hidden His face from you so that He does not hear." Remember, when you sin, you willfully choose to go outside His will and meet your needs on your own. You intentionally deny His power and wisdom to help you. You are saying with your actions that you don't trust Him. Friend, He will not bless that, and He will not contribute to your disobedience. Therefore, if He has identified some sin in your life, you must turn away from it.

Allow me to give you a common illustration of this. You and I know that God's desire for us is to tithe—to give back a tenth of what we earn in gratefulness for all He has provided for us. He instructs in Malachi 3:10, " 'Bring the whole tithe into the storehouse, so that there may be food in My house, and test Me now in this,' says the LORD of hosts, 'if I will not open for you the windows of heaven and pour out for you a blessing until it overflows.' " Now, imagine there is a fellow who doesn't really trust the Father enough to obey Him by tithing. However, he reads Deuteronomy 8:18, which says, "You shall remember the LORD your God, for it is He who is giving you power to make wealth," and he asks the Father to make him rich.

Will God honor that request? No. In fact, the Lord would do that man a terrible disservice if He did. You see, this man is building up his security in money rather than trusting in the Lord, and Scripture is clear: "No one can serve two masters; for either he will hate the one and love the other, or he will be devoted to one and despise the other. You cannot serve God and wealth" (Matt. 6:24). If the Father were to bless him with more affluence, the man would rely on Him less, not more. Let me be clear: God's promises are meant to bolster our trust in Him, not undermine it. He will not sanction disobedience. So as best as you know how, live in obedience to Him.

Sixth, is the fulfillment of this promise in your life encouraging to others?
As I said before, His wonderful assurances to us should be a vital part of our testimony—a living example of His goodness and grace to those around us. They certainly were for the biblical saints. Romans 15:4 tells us, "Whatever was written in earlier times was written for our instruction, so that through perseverance and the encouragement of the Scriptures we might have hope." In other words, we are able to persevere because we see how God worked through their lives. So as you come upon verses in Scripture you would like to claim, ask, "Would it encourage anyone to know God has done this for me? Would it motivate them to seek Him and experience Him for themselves?"

Finally, does the Holy Spirit bear witness with your spirit that God is pleased?

Has the Holy Spirit confirmed that this promise is for you deep within your soul? As we discussed in the previous chapter, peace with the Father is the fruit of oneness with Him. So when you are claiming an assurance He wants to give you, you will sense a profound confidence and calm in the core of your being.

> If you are straying from His will, you will sense within you something akin to static—you will feel chaotic, confused, frustrated, and irritated.

Remember, the Holy Spirit's responsibility is to prepare and enable you to live out what God has chosen for you (1 Cor. 2:9–16). If you are straying from His will, the Spirit will warn you. You will sense within you something akin to the static you see and hear when the connection is off with your radio or television—it is chaotic, confusing, frustrating, and irritating. It is a nervous, muddled restlessness in your soul, and there is nothing good about it. But if you are walking in the center of His will and have a promise He wants you to claim, you will have peace, quietness, and confidence. This doesn't mean you will never face any doubts or fears—we all do at times. Rather, it means that when you are in the Father's presence, He will restore that tranquility to your heart by reminding you of all He has committed to you.

Now this list would not be complete without a gentle word of admonition. As you consider all these questions and your particular situation, please remember that God is absolutely unlimited and sovereign—you cannot put Him in a box or try to control Him. You cannot manipulate Him by saying, "Lord, this is what You said, and I am not going to believe You until it comes to pass." In doing so, you are not exhibiting the heart of faith that honors Him. Rather, you are trying Him, which is clearly prohibited by Scripture because it says, "You shall not put the LORD your God to the test" (Deut. 6:16).

Instead, in all circumstances, recall that the Lord is the sovereign

God of all creation, and He can do as He pleases (Ps. 115:3). If He does not confirm an assurance to you, or if you fail to carry out the conditions of a particular promise, He is not obliged to keep it. But do not be discouraged. As I've explained before, the good news is that whenever He says "No" to you, it is most likely because He has something much better planned.

EXAMPLE 1: PHILIPPIANS 4:19

With that said, I think it would be beneficial to give you a couple of illustrations of how you can go about claiming a promise and applying it to your situation with confidence.

For example, imagine an individual is laid off from his occupation and he turns to the Father for assurance, hope, comfort, and direction. He wants to know that the Lord is actively intervening in his life. So he claims Philippians 4:19, which is often a favorite promise in Scripture that people turn to, "My God will supply all your needs according to His riches in glory in Christ Jesus."

Let us examine this assurance. The Lord will supply all our what? *Needs.* So the first assessment this person must make in considering whether or not this promise applies to his situation is, "Is what I'm asking for really a *need?*" A *need* is something that you require for living or that is essential to your existence. Of course, a job would undoubtedly fit this definition. This man has bills to pay and a household to maintain; he must purchase food and resources. A trade is vital to his survival.

So he goes on to the second consideration, which is whether this promise is *limited* or *general.* Does it relate only to a specific person in history or is it relevant to his particular situation? Thankfully, he realizes from its context that Philippians 4:19 is intended for all believers.

However, as he is examining the verse, he realizes that it is *conditional*—there is a requirement for its fulfillment. He must be "in Christ Jesus," which means that Christ has to be the priority of his life.

And as he looks to Jesus to be his Provider, he must be willing to do whatever the Savior calls him to endeavor—walking in the center of God's plan for his life.

This is why we need to be very careful about how we appropriate promises and the expectations we place on God when we claim them. Philippians 4:19 is not a blank check for whatever we may desire; there are prerequisites associated with it. Rather, it is because of our relationship with Jesus and as we walk in faithful submission to His will that He will meet our every need.

EXAMPLE 2: PSALM 37:4

But say that what a person asks for is not a need; instead, it is a desire. There's a believer and he wants to buy a new car. Now, this is not a request that is critical for his survival—his old automobile has not been in an accident, broken down, or been destroyed in any way. It may be getting a little older and he may be tired of driving it, but it is still a usable form of transportation. So he understands that Philippians 4:19 no longer applies as a promise because a new car is not essential to his existence. Rather, it is simply a purchase that would bring him enjoyment and pleasure.

Of course, there is nothing wrong or sinful with asking God for blessings. The Father takes great joy and pleasure in meeting the desires that fit His will for our lives. In fact, Psalm 37:4 says, "Delight yourself in the LORD; and He will give you the desires of your heart." This is a wonderful promise which most of us have claimed at one point or another. But when is it appropriate for us to petition for it?

Right away we see that though Psalm 37:4 is a *general* promise, it is also *conditional*. The requirement given is that God must rule our hearts and be the focus of our lives. We find our joy in Him. We love Him and enjoy spending time in His presence—reading His Word, worshiping at His throne, and seeking Him in prayer. He is our strength and comfort in times of adversity. In other words, the Father satisfies our needs, and our relationship with Him is the source of our profound contentment, peace, hope, and gladness.

If Jesus is all that to us, that eliminates many of the desires we would normally request, doesn't it? We wouldn't need to ask for anything that would usually give us a sense of self-worth, identity, belonging, competence, honor, or security because we would find all those things in Him.

So let's go back to our example. This man wants to buy a new car, and he is financially able to afford it, so he prays, "Lord, I've been asking You for direction about whether or not to purchase a new vehicle. You said that if I delight myself in You, You would give me my heart's desires. I realize that I don't really need this new car; it's just something I would like to have if You would be so gracious to give it. So please bless me with wisdom and lead me in the way I should go. Amen."

At that point, the Holy Spirit pierces the man's heart with a question, "Why do you really want this car? What is your true motive?" Certainly, the man would be wise to pray through each of the questions I outlined previously and invite the Lord to sift his reasons (Ps. 139:23–24). And perhaps God would highlight some areas of weakness within him.

- Is it because your friend has a new automobile and you want to impress him?
- Is it because you think it will improve your self-worth or help you feel better about yourself?
- Is it because the vehicle, in some way, represents security to you?
- Is it because you believe people will respect you more if you have a finer automobile?
- Is it because having a new car somehow feeds your pride?
- Is it because you have lust, jealousy, or greed in your heart?

If the man wanted that car in order to assuage a need that should be satisfied in God or if it somehow fed a sinful attitude, then Psalm 37:4 would not apply to his request. It couldn't because the man would be violating the one condition necessary for the promise—that he would first delight himself in the Lord.

Therefore, it is extremely important for you to test your motives whenever it comes to God's promises, just as it is as you wait for Him to answer your prayers and fulfill your heart's desires. The Father loves to bless you. But if that longing replaces Him in any way, satiates the needs only He can satisfy, or becomes an idol in your life, He will not compete with it. And if you refuse to wait for Him to provide, then you will undoubtedly miss His very best.

If you refuse to wait for God to provide, then you will undoubtedly miss His very best.

There was a time when the Father taught me this very clearly, and interestingly enough, it likewise involved the purchase of a vehicle.

Several years ago, I was in a terrible accident that wrecked my automobile—someone crashed into me from behind and knocked me thirty-five feet down the road. As I was riding to the hospital in the ambulance, God spoke to me very clearly: "Do not buy another car." I thought this was very odd. I was not hurt too badly, but the only thing I was really focused on was getting my injuries treated in the emergency room. I wasn't interested in even thinking about another vehicle. But His command was so strong that I could not ignore it. "Do not buy another car." Immediately, I realized that He wanted to teach me an important principle, so I obeyed Him.

I waited more than a year. My children kept asking me, "Dad, when are you going to get a car?" And I kept telling them that I was waiting for God to show me what to do.

During that time, someone was very kind to me and lent me a vehicle. I was exceedingly grateful for it, even though the college students gave me a terrible time about its condition and made fun of me whenever they saw it. You see, this loaner was one of those old, beat-up, gas-guzzling Cadillacs with fins that you rarely see anymore. Also, it was enormous—long and clunky, with checkered seats and its own zip code. I was so embarrassed about being seen in it that I would hold my hand up to my face at the stoplight so people wouldn't recognize me. Whenever I would see those college kids, they would say, "Dr. Stanley, you really need a new car!" Still, I thanked God for the transportation.

As I said, I lived this way for more than a year. Finally, the wait and the ridicule got to be too much for me. I gave in to my desire to buy a new vehicle and went down to a local dealership. There was a car there that was all right. It was modest, not pretentious by any means. I test-drove it three times, never feeling quite right about it. In fact, I can remember sitting in the lot of that dealership, staring at the dashboard with my hands on the steering wheel, and thinking, "God, I know You said, 'Don't buy a car,' but I am so embarrassed about driving that old Cadillac. I need to have something respectable to get around in. I guess this is what I ought to do. I should just buy this one."

Again, the Lord spoke to me in a manner I will never forget: "Do you want this or do you want My best?"

I sighed. There was no question in my mind about that. So I replied, "Father, I want Your best. I'm going to trust You," and I got out of the car.

The salesman was standing there. He smiled hopefully and asked, "Well, are you going to take it?"

"No," I responded.

He was very surprised. "Well, why not?"

I just shook my head and said, "Sir, you wouldn't understand." And I left.

It was a week or two later that I rode with a church member to an important meeting. I didn't know him all that well, but he offered to pick me up and take me. So I went, glad to have the opportunity to spend some time with him.

Along the way he asked, "So Charles, when are you going to get yourself a car?"

I thought to myself, *Oh goodness, not this again*. But I managed to reply, "Well, I don't know. God just hasn't given me permission to buy one yet for some reason."

"What would you choose if you could get anything you wanted?" he inquired.

The words were out of my mouth before I could even think about it, "One just like this," I said. This man had a very fine vehicle, one far superior than I had ever considered purchasing for myself. So I have no idea why I responded that way. But apparently God did.

Three days later, I received a check to buy an automobile just like his—a car far better than I had hoped for or could have imagined. And it was absolutely free.

I was certainly grateful that when I was tempted to purchase that inferior vehicle after more than a year of waiting that I listened to God and didn't do it. It would have been a terrible mistake. But because I obeyed the Lord, I received a wonderful blessing. I didn't ask for or expect it, but my loving heavenly Father provided it for me anyway.

Friend, God never fails to show us His grace, goodness, love, and mercy when we wait for Him. This is why I beseech you—delight yourself in the Lord, make Him the priority of your life, wait for Him, cling to His promises, and trust Him to give you the desires of your heart. He knows your needs and longings even better than you do, and He wants to fulfill them in a manner that reveals the awesome way He loves and provides for you.

> God never fails to show us His grace, goodness, love, and mercy when we wait for Him.

I understand the pressures you feel. I know what it is like to be embarrassed. I've experienced the confusion, emptiness, and doubt that arise when it appears the Father will never answer your prayers. But when I say that He gives us "infinitely beyond our highest prayers, desires, thoughts, or hopes" (Eph. 3:20, TLB), it is because I have seen Him do so firsthand, and not just this time with the car, but over and over again throughout my life.

YOUR PART IN THE PROMISE

With that said, no matter what promise you are claiming from God and regardless of what you feel you need or desire, you have three responsibilities when it comes to that assurance being fulfilled in your life. You play a crucial part in seeing it come to fruition, and that is: You must exhibit faith, patience, and obedience as you wait for the Lord to accomplish it. You must allow God to do things His way.

Recall what we read in Hebrews 10:35–36, "Do not throw away your confidence, which has a great reward. For you have need of endurance, so that when you have done the will of God, you may receive what was promised." Let's break this down.

The first point is, "Do not throw away your confidence, which has a great reward." That is, you must hold on to your *faith*, or the confident conviction God will do as He's promised. Remember, "Without faith it is impossible to please Him, for he who comes to God must believe that He is and that He is a rewarder of those who seek Him" (Heb. 11:6). Therefore, when the Father has given you a promise, you must set your heart to fully believe that He is able and willing to fulfill it in your life. Everything may fight against your faith in Him—all of your senses, your understanding, even the way your circumstances appear—but trust Him anyway, and your confidence in Him will grow.

The second admonishment is, "You have need of endurance." That is, you need *patience*, which is represented by two words in the New Testament. The first one, *makrothumeo*, signifies our long-suffering attitude toward others and suggests the ability to be wronged and not retaliate. The second term, however, *hupomone*, means, "steadfastness, constancy, and perseverance." It applies to difficult circumstances and is the picture of a believer who does not stray from the course that Christ has set, despite obstacles and trials.

Now, perseverance does not usually come naturally to us, it is not generally a trait we are born with. We typically prefer to have what we want right away. Rather, it is a characteristic that must be developed through adversity. And so, just as with faith, we must *choose* to be patient. We must make the decision to endure and stay in the center of God's will no matter how long it takes for Him to fulfill the promise.

Nineteenth-century South African pastor and writer Andrew Murray explains, "It is resting in the Lord, in His will, His promise, His faithfulness, and His love, that makes patience easy."[1] Therefore, fix your eyes on Jesus so you will be able to persevere and attain what He's promised (Heb. 12:1–2).

> Obediently allow Him to guide you step-by-step to your desired destination.

The final condition is, "When you have done the will of God, you may receive what was promised." In other words, you must be *obedient*—you must submit to Him. You must allow Him to guide you step-by-step to your desired destination, whether you understand His direction to you or not. Why? Because only He knows the best way to fulfill that promise in your life. And when you truly trust that He is God, you believe that He knows how to lead you on the path to the promise better than anyone on earth, even yourself. You have absolute confidence that whatever He commands you to do is for your good and His glory.

Friend, do not live in promise poverty. Endure this time of waiting victoriously by actively taking hold of the wonderful assurances He has given you in Scripture. Believe He will help you. Trust that He has great plans for your life and better blessings than you can imagine. And have faith that when you have steadfastly and patiently obeyed Him, He will provide for you powerfully just as He did all those who have gone before you (Heb. 6:11–12).

Father, how grateful I am for the precious and magnificent promises You give me in Your Word. Truly, You are good and tenderhearted to those who seek You and comfort those who wait for You. Thank You for revealing Your will to me and for always helping me to endure. Teach me to actively claim Your promises and obey You step-by-step in this season of delay. You are so powerful, wise, and true, so trustworthy and reliable. Thank You for keeping Your word throughout history. And thank You, Father, for having special promises appropriated just for me and for keeping them so faithfully.

Lord, I want You to rule my heart and be the focus of my life. I long to find my joy in You. I yearn to spend time worshiping in Your wonderful presence—with a passion for Your Word and a heart for prayer. You are my strength, comfort, and hope in times of adversity. You are the source of my life, my delight, my peace, and my all.

Father, I want to trust You wholeheartedly—with a strong, vibrant, and unshakable faith. Teach me to be patient and wise, steadfastly remaining on the path You've set for me regardless of how long it takes or the obstacles I encounter. Keep me in the center of Your will, obediently following and honoring You even when I do not see that way ahead. I put my hope in You, my Lord and my Savior. Thank You for drawing me closer to You, for working in the unseen on my behalf, and for preparing blessings for me that are infinitely beyond my best dreams, highest aspirations, and dearest desires. In Your holy and wonderful name I pray, Lord Jesus. Amen.

POINTS FOR ACTIVE WAITING

1. Memorize Hebrews 10:23, "Let us hold fast the confession
    of our hope without wavering, for He who promised is
    faithful."
2. Whenever you feel anxious because of this season of delay,
    repeat Hebrews 10:23, Philippians 2:13, Proverbs 3:5–6,
    Psalm 62:5–6, and Psalm 27:14 to yourself.
3. Are there promises that are important to you? Spend time
    reading Scripture and asking the Father to reveal the assur-
    ances He desires for you to claim. As you come upon verses
    that are meaningful to you, ask the Lord if they are promises
    you can appropriate or principles you should practice. If you
    need help knowing whether or not they are meant for you,
    review the questions that begin on page 138 for clarification.
    Whenever God identifies a promise He wants you to take
    hold of, be sure to write it in the space provided or in your
    journal, memorize it, and refer to it often to build your faith.
4. As a believer, you are spiritually wealthy because of the
    exceedingly great promises you have in Jesus. Below are
    some of the wonderful ways the Father answers your deep-
    est needs and assurances you can claim as your own. Read
    through this list whenever you need encouragement and
    remember to thank God daily for all the ways He has pro-
    vided for you.

NEED	PROMISE
RECONCILIATION WITH GOD	God demonstrates His own love toward us, in that while we were yet sinners, Christ died for us. Much more then, having now been justified by His blood, we shall be saved from the wrath of God through Him. For if while we were enemies we were reconciled to God through the death of His Son, much more, having been reconciled, we shall be saved by His life. —Romans 5:8–10
GOD'S LOVE	Neither death, nor life, nor angels, nor principalities, nor things present, nor things to come, nor powers, nor height, nor depth, nor any other created thing, will be able to separate us from the love of God, which is in Christ Jesus our Lord. —Romans 8:38–39
ASSURANCE OF SALVATION	My sheep hear My voice, and I know them, and they follow Me; and I give eternal life to them, and they will never perish; and no one will snatch them out of My hand. My Father, who has given them to Me, is greater than all; and no one is able to snatch them out of the Father's hand. I and the Father are one. —John 10:27–30
ACCEPTANCE BY GOD	See how great a love the Father has bestowed on us, that we would be called children of God; and such we are. —1 John 3:1
GOD'S PRESENCE	The Lord is the one who goes ahead of you; He will be with you. He will not fail you or forsake you. Do not fear or be dismayed. —Deuteronomy 31:8
BENEFIT OF WAITING	Those who wait for the Lord will gain new strength; they will mount up with wings like eagles, they will run and not get tired, they will walk and not become weary. —Isaiah 40:31

NEED	PROMISE
HOPEFULNESS FOR TIMES OF WAITING	From days of old they have not heard or perceived by ear, nor has the eye seen a God besides You, who acts in behalf of the one who waits for Him. —Isaiah 64:4
GUARANTEE OF WAITING	The vision is yet for the appointed time; it hastens toward the goal and it will not fail. Though it tarries, wait for it; for it will certainly come, it will not delay. —Habakkuk 2:3
THE SECURITY OF WAITING ON GOD	The Lord is good to those who wait for Him, to the person who seeks Him. It is good that he waits silently for the salvation of the Lord. —Lamentations 3:25–26
THE COURAGE TO WAIT	My soul, wait in silence for God only, for my hope is from Him. He only is my rock and my salvation, my stronghold; I shall not be shaken. —Psalm 62:5–6
CONFIDENCE IN TIMES OF ANXIETY	Do not fear, for I am with you; do not anxiously look about you, for I am your God. I will strengthen you, surely I will help you, surely I will uphold you with My righteous right hand. —Isaiah 41:10
PROTECTION	"No weapon that is formed against you will prosper; And every tongue that accuses you in judgment you will condemn. This is the heritage of the servants of the Lord, And their vindication is from Me," declares the Lord. —Isaiah 54:17
PROVISION	My God will supply all your needs according to His riches in glory in Christ Jesus. —Philippians 4:19
STRENGTH	I can do all things through Him who strengthens me. —Philippians 4:13

NEED	PROMISE
THE INDWELLING COUNSEL AND HELP OF THE HOLY SPIRIT	I will ask the Father, and He will give you another Helper, that He may be with you forever. —John 14:16
GUIDANCE	I will instruct you and teach you in the way which you should go; I will counsel you with My eye upon you. —Psalm 32:8
WISDOM FOR EVERY CHALLENGE	If any of you lacks wisdom, let him ask of God, who gives to all generously and without reproach, and it will be given to him. —James 1:5
ANSWERS TO PRAYER	This is the confidence which we have before Him, that, if we ask anything according to His will, He hears us. And if we know that He hears us in whatever we ask, we know that we have the requests which we have asked from Him. —1 John 5:14–15
BLESSING	The Lord God is a sun and shield; the Lord gives grace and glory; no good thing does He withhold from those who walk uprightly. —Psalm 84:11
THE DESIRE OF YOUR HEART	Delight yourself in the Lord; and He will give you the desires of your heart. —Psalm 37:4
HELP WITH BURDENS	Blessed be the Lord, who daily bears our burden, the God who is our salvation. —Psalm 68:19
COMFORT IN DISTRESS	Blessed be the God and Father of our Lord Jesus Christ, the Father of mercies and God of all comfort, who comforts us in all our affliction so that we will be able to comfort those who are in any affliction with the comfort with which we ourselves are comforted by God. —2 Corinthians 1:3–4

NEED	PROMISE
REFUGE IN TIMES OF TROUBLE	God is our refuge and strength, a very present help in trouble. Therefore we will not fear, though the earth should change and though the mountains slip into the heart of the sea. —Psalm 46:1–2
FORGIVENESS OF SINS	If we confess our sins, He is faithful and righteous to forgive us our sins and to cleanse us from all unrighteousness. —1 John 1:9
DELIVERANCE FROM TEMPTATION	No temptation has overtaken you but such as is common to man; and God is faithful, who will not allow you to be tempted beyond what you are able, but with the temptation will provide the way of escape also, so that you will be able to endure it. —1 Corinthians 10:13
REST FOR THE SOUL	Come to Me, all who are weary and heavy-laden, and I will give you rest. Take My yoke upon you and learn from Me, for I am gentle and humble in heart, and you will find rest for your souls. —Matthew 11:28–29
PEACE	Be anxious for nothing, but in everything by prayer and supplication with thanksgiving let your requests be made known to God. And the peace of God, which surpasses all comprehension, will guard your hearts and your minds in Christ Jesus. —Philippians 4:6–7
FRUITFULNESS	The righteous man will flourish like the palm tree, he will grow like a cedar in Lebanon. Planted in the house of the Lord, they will flourish in the courts of our God. They will still yield fruit in old age; they shall be full of sap and very green, to declare that the Lord is upright; He is my rock, and there is no unrighteousness in Him. —Psalm 92:12–15

NEED	PROMISE
HEALING	Bless the Lord, O my soul, and forget none of His benefits; who pardons all your iniquities, who heals all your diseases. —Psalm 103:2–3
AN ETERNAL HOME IN HEAVEN	Do not let your heart be troubled; believe in God, believe also in Me. In My Father's house are many dwelling places; if it were not so, I would have told you; for I go to prepare a place for you. If I go and prepare a place for you, I will come again and receive you to Myself, that where I am, there you may be also. —John 14:1–3

Use this space to respond to the "Points for Active Waiting" and to record prayer requests, key lessons God is teaching you, and your insights about waiting on the Lord to act on your behalf.

_____

_____

_____

_____

_____

_____

_____

_____

_____

_____

_____

_____

_____

_____

_____

_____

_____

_____

_____

_____

_____

_____

_____

Be strong and courageous,
do not be afraid or tremble at them,
for the LORD your God is the one who goes with you.
He will not fail you or forsake you.
—Deuteronomy 31:6

6

STAYING ON TRACK
WHEN THE VIEW BECOMES DARK
Surviving the Wait with Courage

We've been talking about focusing on God, discovering His will, and claiming His promises in order to make the most of our seasons of waiting. But the truth of the matter is that the delays can continue to be absolutely disheartening, especially when circumstances still do not go your way or your burdens get heavier. And in the midst of your waiting times, moments may arise when all hope looks to be utterly gone and lost forever. We will confront these instances now, so you will be prepared to handle them as they emerge. From all appearances, it may seem to you as if the Lord will never come through for you. What can you do when all around you is dark and foreboding, with no visible signs of reprieve? What can possibly restore your courage and confidence?

Most likely, you have experienced these heartbreaking occasions before—the devastating disappointments that rob the last of your strength and resolution. The days go by without any answers to your prayers, then the months, and maybe even the years. The illness, financial difficulty, conflict, loneliness, uncertainty, or need persists. And then more obstacles appear: a bad medical report, unexpected expenses, disagreements, setbacks you couldn't have foreseen, and more crushing pressures. The least words of criticism or unbelief from another person send you reeling with hopelessness because they confirm your worst fears. Everything has gone so wrong. You wonder, *Is this my life now? Is this it forever?* You struggle, feeling the overwhelming temptation to give in to utter despair and fall back into destructive habits: addictions, overspending, overeating, gossip, sexual sins, self-condemnation, or what have you. Sometimes you lose the fight, which leaves you feeling even more unworthy of God's good gifts.

Your situation seems to be getting worse, not better, not in the least. You wake up day after day trying to stir up the determination to continue pressing forward. But in your heart you feel as if there is no way you can go on and no reason to try.

I imagine that is how James Cash Penney felt when he lost $40 million in the stock market crash of 1929 and became deathly ill from the overwhelming stress of his circumstances. Seven million dollars in arrears and false accusations of fiscal impropriety lodged against him, Penney's world was shaken in a way few will know. All his hope, security, and everything he'd worked for so diligently his entire life was not only irreversibly gone, but he was being persecuted because of it. He had absolutely no way to pay back the mountainous debts he owed.

> "No matter what may be the test, God will take care of you; lean, weary one, upon His breast, God will take care of you."
> —C. D. MARTIN

After two years of unsuccessfully pouring every ounce of courage and energy into trying to overcome his difficulties, he was done. He had nothing left to give and even less to live for. The emotionally and physically spent Penney wrote, "I was convinced I would never see another dawn. I wrote farewell letters to my family. Then I waited for the end—a failure at the age of 56."[6]

Although Penney felt as if he had no future, God had other plans. One day at the Battle Creek Sanitarium in Michigan,[7] where he was being treated for his despair, Penney heard the hymn, "God Will Take Care of You" by Civilla D. Martin, which says,

Be not dismayed whate'er betide,
God will take care of you;
Beneath His wings of love abide,
God will take care of you.

Refrain: *God will take care of you,*
Through every day, over all the way;
He will take care of you,
God will take care of you.

Through days of toil when heart doth fail,
God will take care of you;
When dangers fierce your path assail,
God will take care of you.

All you may need He will provide,
God will take care of you;
Nothing you ask will be denied,
God will take care of you.

No matter what may be the test,
God will take care of you;
Lean, weary one, upon His breast,
God will take care of you.[8]

It was the glimmer of hope he needed. Penney decided to trust the Lord Jesus as his Savior. And not only did he survive his overwhelming difficulties, but he also lived to be ninety-five, built a tremendous financial empire through his JCPenney® stores, and was a great philanthropist who helped countless people.

Understand, Penney grew up in the household of a Baptist pastor. He lived by Christian principles throughout his life. But this was the point Jesus became *real* to him. He could testify—as did the adversity-stricken

Job—"I know that You can do all things, and that no purpose of Yours can be thwarted. . . . I have heard of You by the hearing of the ear; but now my eye sees You" (Job 42:2, 5). In other words, he realized what we discussed in Chapter 2—that the Lord is indeed GOD. Penney testified, "I felt the power of God as I had never felt it before."

It was in this state of complete brokenness that Penney discovered he did not need to be strong, capable, self-sufficient, or perfect, because the Lord Jesus had already become all these things for him. Therefore, this low point in Penney's life was not an end. Rather, it was a new beginning—a dawn of greater endeavors that the Father had planned for him all along.

As you read this today, perhaps you are experiencing devastating difficulties or are aware of impending challenges on the horizon that seem to trample every hope you have. You've been trying to set your focus on the Father, wholeheartedly—and maybe even tearfully—pursuing His will and claiming His promises. But the discouragement still overwhelms you. This is because there is nothing that can plunge you into the darkness of despair like a prolonged time of waiting with no end in view. You may wrestle constantly with whether or not you need to give up on your goals and dreams because you feel like you don't measure up and will never deserve the good gifts you desire. You wonder why the Lord doesn't change your heart or at least make the rest of your life easier to manage as you wait. But He doesn't.

Each night you go to bed thinking, "Oh God, please—no more delays." But the pressures persist. Why? Where is the Lord in all this? Why does He allow His children to face such dark moments?

This brings us to the fourth and final requirement of waiting on the Lord, which is *courage*. Recall our definition: Waiting on the Lord signifies an expectant endurance that is demonstrated by a *directed, purposeful, active,* and *courageous* attitude of prayer. *Courage* is a quality that enables us to endure suffering, danger, opposition, and the challenges of life steadfastly, fearlessly, and with confidence in God's provision and protection. It is this attribute of courage that is stretched and refined in these painful times.

It is not easy to be courageous, especially in the darkest of moments when we are shaken to the core of our being. But courage is a state of mind that is absolutely essential for the child of God to triumph. When everything looks bleak and there is no hope in view, we dauntlessly continue to trust that the Father is in complete control. We don't give up or quit because we have faith that the Lord is still God and He has a wonderful plan for our lives. And we are willing to face adversity and forgo good opportunities that offer temporary comfort in order to take hold of the very best the Lord has planned for us.

So how can you stay on track with His purposes for your life when everything seems so dark and you feel so desolate? And how can you bravely take hold of the truth that "God will take care of you," like James Cash Penney did?

To answer these questions, let us look at the life of one of the great leaders in Scripture—Joseph, a young man who understood walking through darkness with courage and determination. For thirteen years he waited through increasingly worsening conditions until God raised him up to be one of the most important figures in Jewish history.

WALKING WITH GOD THROUGH THE DARKNESS

Perhaps you recall Joseph's story. From early on, he appeared to be a bright and promising young man. Although he was one of thirteen—his father Jacob had twelve boys and one girl—Joseph certainly stood out among his siblings. Unfortunately, this was not always a good thing. Genesis 37 tells us,

> Israel [also called Jacob] loved Joseph more than all his sons, because he was the son of his old age; and he made him a varicolored tunic.

His brothers saw that their father loved him more than all his brothers; and so they hated him and could not speak to him on friendly
terms. Then Joseph had a dream, and when he told it to his brothers,
they hated him even more. He said to them, "Please listen to this
dream which I have had; for behold, we were binding sheaves in the
field, and lo, my sheaf rose up and also stood erect; and behold, your
sheaves gathered around and bowed down to my sheaf." Then his
brothers said to him, "Are you actually going to reign over us? Or are
you really going to rule over us?" So they hated him even more for his
dreams and for his words. (vv. 3–8)

This was where Joseph's trouble began. Some of it, of course, he
brought on himself. It wasn't necessarily the wisest choice for him to
share that dream. But perhaps you can understand what it's like to grow
up in a household where you are the outcast and you feel compelled to
prove your worthiness. Yes, his father and mother loved him, but the
majority of Joseph's family despised him. Imagine having all those
brothers accusing, mocking, and criticizing him constantly. No matter
what Joseph did, they rejected him—he was
never right, never good enough, and never acceptable. He must have felt terribly inadequate
and unwanted.

Joseph bravely
made the best of
his circumstances,
worked hard,
and was very
disciplined.

In fact, the animosity between Joseph and
his brothers went so deep that they "plotted
against him to put him to death" (Gen. 37:18)
and threw him in a pit until they could decide
what to do with him. While the brothers were debating their options,
some Midianite traders came by, pulled Joseph out of the pit, and sold
him to Ishmaelite merchants (Gen. 37:28). They, in turn, took him to
Egypt where he was purchased by Potiphar, the captain of Pharaoh's
royal guard (Gen. 39:1).

Joseph went from being a free man among family to a slave in a foreign country where he didn't know anyone and had no understanding

of the language or customs. But instead of blaming his brothers for his misfortunes, Joseph bravely made the best of his circumstances, worked hard, and was very disciplined. In fact, Joseph excelled at all he did and became a favorite of Potiphar's, who appeared to be a fair and reasonable master. Genesis 39:4–6 reports,

> Joseph found favor in his sight and became his personal servant; and [Potiphar] made him overseer over his house, and all that he owned he put in his charge. It came about that from the time he made him overseer in his house and over all that he owned, the LORD blessed the Egyptian's house on account of Joseph; thus the LORD's blessing was upon all that he owned, in the house and in the field. So he left everything he owned in Joseph's charge.

Joseph did very well in Potiphar's service, at least for a time. Sadly, Joseph's success there was short-lived as well. Potiphar's wife saw that Joseph was a handsome young man and attempted to seduce him. Another man may have yielded to the temptation, but Joseph was a faithful Hebrew who was devoted to the Lord. He rejected her advances, saying, "My master trusts me with everything in his entire household. No one here has more authority than I do. He has held back nothing from me except you, because you are his wife. How could I do such a wicked thing? It would be a great sin against God" (Gen. 39:8–9, NLT).

Though Joseph acted honorably, this woman was infuriated that he refused her. So she framed him and had him sent to jail (Gen. 39:20). The entire situation was absolutely unjust. Of course, if Joseph had been a different kind of person, he easily could have been eaten alive by bitterness, unforgiveness, and doubts of the Lord's goodness. After all, he'd done what was right and was incarcerated for it. He'd gone from a free man to a favored servant to a prison inmate, even though he had done nothing wrong.

He could have seethed with resentful thoughts as most people do: *Why has all this evil come upon me? Where is God in all this? Why didn't*

He stop my brothers or Mrs. Potiphar from being so cruel to me? What did I do to deserve this? Has the Lord forgotten what He revealed to me in my dreams? But he didn't. Instead, Joseph acted courageously—choosing to trust in the Lord. And because he did so, Joseph's story does not end here. When the time was right, God honored him greatly.

But what I want you to take note of here is that while Joseph was in prison, he again exhibited faith by working hard and making the best of his situation. And because of it, the Father blessed him. Genesis 39:21–23 reports, "The Lord was with Joseph and extended kindness to him, and gave him favor in the sight of the chief jailer. The chief jailer committed to Joseph's charge all the prisoners who were in the jail; so that whatever was done there, he was responsible for it. The chief jailer did not supervise anything under Joseph's charge because the Lord was with him; and whatever he did, the Lord made to prosper."

GOD IS WITH YOU

Did you notice how many times Scripture spoke of the Father's presence with Joseph? Repeatedly throughout this narrative of Joseph's life, we read:

- "The Lord was with Joseph, so he became a successful man" (Gen. 39:2).
- "His master saw that the Lord was with him and how the Lord caused all that he did to prosper in his hand" (Gen. 39:3).
- "The Lord blessed the Egyptian's house on account of Joseph" (Gen. 39:5).
- "The Lord was with Joseph and extended kindness to him" (Gen. 39:21).
- "The chief jailer did not supervise anything under Joseph's charge because the Lord was with him; and whatever he did, the Lord made to prosper" (Gen. 39:23).

Even Joseph was able to say, "God has made me fruitful in the land of my affliction" (Gen. 41:52). I believe one of the important reasons Joseph was able to maintain his courage, dignity, and optimism through such severe circumstances was because he was aware of the Father's presence with him through it all, no matter how dismal the situation appeared.

Therefore, this is the first point that will be crucial for you to remember as the adversity persists: *You can be courageous because the Lord is with you in the darkest of times and will see you through them.*

Let me repeat: *The Father is with you even in the dark times.* It's very important that we remember this, because when we encounter times of waiting, we often feel utterly alone and rejected. We imagine that even the Lord has abandoned us. Because of this, we assess ourselves as unworthy of anything good—even the blessings God has promised us—and figure that our worthlessness must be the reason He is tarrying and has not yet helped us.

There may be something in your life that makes you think the Father couldn't love or bless you—perhaps it is a bad decision, remnants of past abuse, a particular failing, or an event in your past that seems insurmountable. But friend, nothing can separate you from God's love (Rom. 8:38–39). In fact, Scripture testifies that it's when you feel at your most unworthy and defeated that the Father is closest to you. Psalm 34:18 promises, "The LORD is near to the brokenhearted and saves those who are crushed in spirit." God's Word is replete with assurances that He never abandons you:

- "The LORD is the one who goes ahead of you; He will be with you. He will not fail you or forsake you. Do not fear or be dismayed" (Deut. 31:8).

- "Be strong and courageous! Do not tremble or be dismayed, for the LORD your God is with you wherever you go" (Josh. 1:9).
- "Do not fear, for I am with you; do not anxiously look about you, for I am your God. I will strengthen you, surely I will help you, surely I will uphold you with My righteous right hand" (Isa. 41:10).
- " 'They shall call His name Immanuel,' which translated means, 'God with us' " (Matt. 1:23).
- "Lo, I am with you always, even to the end of the age" (Matt. 28:20).
- "I will not leave you as orphans; I will come to you" (John 14:18).
- "He Himself has said, 'I WILL NEVER DESERT YOU, NOR WILL I EVER FORSAKE YOU' " (Heb. 13:5).
- And many more. In fact, if this is an area you struggle with, it may be worthwhile for you to look up: Deuteronomy 31:6; Joshua 1:5; Psalm 23:4; Psalm 46:10–11; Psalm 73:23–24; Psalm 139:7–10; Isaiah 43:1–2; Jeremiah 15:20; Zephaniah 3:17; Romans 8:35–39; and 2 Timothy 4:16–18.

God has not and will not abandon you. He knows exactly where you are and what you are facing during this dark time and He is walking with you in it, whether you sense His presence or not. It is a fact—He is still your Protector and Provider in the midst of this situation. Therefore, whenever you begin to feel afraid, alone, rejected, unwanted, or unworthy during this season of delay, remember that the Lord is with you, He has not deserted you, and He will never forsake you.

Likewise, the reason Joseph prospered was because God blessed the work of his hands. It was not because Joseph was more wise, skilled, or talented than the other servants. Rather, it was because "the LORD caused all that he did to prosper" (Gen. 39:3).

The same is true for you—it is God who makes you triumph. Sadly, a frequent by-product of feeling unwanted or abandoned is how unworthy it makes us feel of other blessings. We may not even realize that this is the case. But because of rejection by a parent, a loved one, an authority figure, or what have you, we doubt our value, identity, abilities, and usefulness. We may even come to feel we don't deserve to be successful or have our dearest prayers answered. But Scripture is clear, "Our adequacy is from God" (2 Cor. 3:5). It is Jesus our Savior who makes us worthy of His blessings (Eph. 1:3).

Therefore, when you are especially disheartened during your times of waiting, it is crucial for you to remember—always hold this truth close—that it is not what or who you know; the intelligence, strength, beauty, or power you hold; or what you've achieved in life that matters. Your heart's desires do not hinge on you being "good enough." Rather, it is the Spirit of the living God in you and how much of your life He actively influences that will cause you to succeed (Zech. 4:6; Phil. 2:13).

This was certainly true of King David. Was he the brightest, most handsome, or most able of all his brothers? No. In fact, his father, Jesse, didn't even bother to call David in from tending the sheep when the prophet Samuel asked to see all his sons (1 Sam. 16:11). The youngest of the household, David must not have seemed very impressive next to his seven older brothers.

But remember what the Lord told Samuel as he reviewed David's eldest brother, Eliab, "Do not look at his appearance or at the height of his stature, because I have rejected him; for God sees not as man sees, for man looks at the outward appearance, but the LORD looks at the heart" (1 Sam. 16:9). It was David's love and dedication to God that made him extraordinary and eventually qualified him to be king of Israel.

The same was true of the disciples. They were not the brightest and best that Israel had to offer—most of them were just simple, unschooled fishermen. They did not have any wealth, training, manners, influence, or pedigree to recommend them. Yet people could see Jesus shining through them in a profound, inspiring way that was absolutely unmistakable.

In fact, even the religious leaders of the day, who represented the most distinguished minds and had the greatest advantages of the

Jewish people, acknowledged the power of the disciples' words. Acts 4:13 reports, "As they observed the confidence of Peter and John and understood that they were uneducated and untrained men, they were amazed, and began to recognize them as having been with Jesus." In other words, it was the Lord shining through them that made them extraordinary (2 Cor. 4:7).

Likewise, you are assured in 2 Chronicles 16:9, "The eyes of the LORD move to and fro throughout the earth that He may strongly support those whose heart is completely His." When you belong to God and actively obey Him, He blesses you. Yes, your circumstances may look somewhat dark right now, but you do not have to be afraid that it's because you are not smart, powerful, beautiful, pious, charismatic, skilled, or sophisticated enough. On the contrary, the adversity you're facing is not about any of that. Rather, it is for your training, which we will discuss further in the next section. And as you submit to the Father during this difficult time, He provides for you, makes you all you need to be, bends other people's hearts toward you, and sets the path for your victory.

> As you submit to the Father during this difficult time, He provides for you, makes you all you need to be, bends other people's hearts toward you, and sets the path for your victory.

Of course, you should always look your best, do your best and be your best as you obediently and faithfully seek God. Doing so honors Him. But as you commit yourself to Him, you can be confident the Lord does the rest. The Father shines through you and makes you more than adequate for whatever lies ahead.

GOD HAS A PURPOSE

At this point, the question that usually arises is, "If God is with me in the darkness and He is omnipotent, then why doesn't He change my circumstances? Why does He allow me to suffer and wait?" This is the second point that you must remember as the difficult times persist: *The Lord has an important purpose for the seasons of adversity you face.*

We can see this as we look at the rest of Joseph's story. When we left Joseph, he was in prison, where he had achieved the favor of the chief jailer. So he was in an excellent position when the Pharaoh's cupbearer and baker were incarcerated and had dreams they needed interpreted.

Genesis 40:6–8 says, "When Joseph came to them in the morning and observed them, behold, they were dejected. He asked Pharaoh's officials who were with him in confinement in his master's house, 'Why are your faces so sad today?' Then they said to him, 'We have had a dream and there is no one to interpret it.' Then Joseph said to them, 'Do not interpretations belong to God? Tell it to me, please.'" The cupbearer did so and Joseph responded, "Within three more days Pharaoh will lift up your head and restore you to your office; and you will put Pharaoh's cup into his hand according to your former custom when you were his cupbearer. Only keep me in mind when it goes well with you, and please do me a kindness by mentioning me to Pharaoh and get me out of this house" (Gen. 40:13–14).

You can imagine the optimism that stirred in Joseph's heart. Finally, he saw a glimmer of hope, a way out of the dungeon. Perhaps the cupbearer would help him and he could be free. Maybe his life could get back on track and those wonderful dreams he'd had could at long last come true.

Sadly, the wait was not yet over for Joseph. The chief cupbearer completely forgot about him for two full years (Gen. 40:23–41:1). One may wonder how long it was before this new delay wore on Joseph's soul as the days and weeks passed without word.

These are the postponements that make the normal person question everything, the disappointments that can send the soul reeling in despair. Once again, the anticipation of a better life seems to be crushed. It appears as if nothing will ever change. As if God has forgotten. As if we are doomed to the desolate state we find ourselves in.

However, these are also the times that make us decide whether or not we truly believe the Lord—whether He is real to us or merely a nice idea we cling to. Do we sincerely have confidence He will work this situation out for our good? Or is our cynicism justified?

The first reason God allows you to endure dark times is to firmly mature and establish your trust in Him when there is no visible evidence of His activity.

During such times, the person with *little faith* will say, "The Lord has promised to help me, and I think He can, but I'm not certain He will."

One with *maturing faith* will testify, "Not only do I know the Father can see me through this dark time, I am sure He will."

But when you and I have *perfect faith*, we are confident that what the Lord has promised is already accomplished—on the other side of this adversity is the wonderful blessing we've yearned for and it will be even more meaningful to us because we've held on to Him through every trial and setback. In fact, I have always believed that the deeper and darker the valley we experience, the greater the blessing the Father has planned for us.

This was certainly true for Joseph. And it is here that we can again glean tremendous hope and encouragement from his story. Joseph held on to his hope and eventually, after two years, the call came for him to shave his face and change his clothes. Pharaoh had a dream that needed interpretation, so the cupbearer told him of the extraordinary man of God he'd met in the dungeon. Impressed, the Pharaoh summoned Joseph (Gen. 41:1–14).

The second reason the Lord allows you to experience seasons of darkness is to prepare you.

The Father readies your character and gets you precisely where you need to be physically, relationally, and spiritually, engineering millions of details to place you exactly where you should be, at the moment it's crucial for you to be there for maximum impact.

Joseph was positioned perfectly and spiritually prepared for what would come next. Pharaoh recounted his disturbing dream to the young Hebrew man. Joseph replied, "God has told to Pharaoh what He is about to do" (Gen. 41:25), and was able to warn the Egyptian king of seven years of plenty and seven years of famine that were coming. Thankfully, because of the insight the Lord had given him, Joseph was also able to suggest a plan that would ultimately save the people of Egypt and his whole family (Gen. 41:14–37).

The Father readies your character and places you exactly where you should be, when you should be there, for maximum impact.

The third reason the Father permits times of darkness in your life is so others can witness His work through you.

Because of all God had done in Joseph's life in those thirteen dark years—testing him, stretching his faith, refining his character, and teaching him faithfully—it was obvious to everyone *Who* was helping this remarkable Hebrew man.

One would rationally surmise that Joseph's imprisonment, his appearance, the false accusations against him, and even the fact that he was a foreigner among the Egyptians would impede his advancement, undermine his credibility, and possibly ruin the rest of his life. But none of it ultimately mattered. Only the Lord's influence on his life stood out.

In fact, Pharaoh proclaimed, "Can we find a man like this, in whom is a divine spirit? . . . Since God has informed you of all this, there is no one so discerning and wise as you are. You shall be over my house, and according to your command all my people shall do homage; only in the throne I will be greater than you" (Gen. 41:38–40). The Lord completely orchestrated the events that allowed Joseph to become the leader of all Egypt, second only to Pharaoh. And everyone knew it.

The fourth reason the Lord allows you to experience extended times of darkness is to raise you up and place you in a position to bless others.

Ultimately, the purpose for this divine and prolonged sequence of events that brought Joseph to Egypt, trained him to be a skilled administrator, and placed him where Pharaoh could utilize his talents was to save the whole world from a devastating famine. Genesis 41:57 reports, "The people of all the earth came to Egypt to buy grain from Joseph, because the famine was severe in all the earth."

Think about how God touched the world through Joseph's life and what an astounding testimony it was to the Father's awesome wisdom, power, and provision to people from every nation, tribe, and tongue. Yes, the Lord changed all of Joseph's circumstances in an instant— taking him from prison to Pharaoh's palace in the twinkling of an eye. But the Father had worked tirelessly on this Hebrew man's character for thirteen years so that when that absolutely crucial moment in history came—when the people would need his God-centered leadership— Joseph would be ready.

The same is true for you. You may not have any idea of how the Lord wants to work through you, especially as you endure this dark time of waiting. Nothing makes sense and everything may appear exceedingly grim. But God *is* preparing you to be a blessing to others.

The fact that you are facing a time of suffering is proof of it. Recall the admonition of 2 Corinthians 1:3–4, "Blessed be the God and Father of our Lord Jesus Christ, the Father of mercies and God of all comfort, who comforts us in all our affliction so that we will be able to comfort those who are in any affliction with the comfort with which we ourselves are comforted by God." In order to make you His useful and effective representative, the Father trains you in the fires of adversity, just as He did Joseph. Why? Because there is nothing that deepens your understanding, stirs your compassion for others, and shows you what is truly important the way pain does.

A. B. Simpson, author and founder of the Christian and Missionary Alliance, explains, "The pressure helps us to understand the trials of others, and fits us to help and sympathize with them. There is a shallow, superficial nature, that gets hold of a theory or a promise lightly, and talks very glibly about the distrust of those who shrink from every trial; but the man or woman who has suffered much never does this, but is very tender and gentle, and knows what suffering really means."[9]

It is the adversity you experience that truly equips you to influence those around you. Therefore, never underestimate the awesome encouragement you can be to another person or the example you set as a follower of Jesus during the difficult times of your life.

I saw this firsthand during one of the most excruciating trials I have ever experienced. It affected absolutely everything in my life. In fact, I thought it would devastate my ministry and undermine what God had called me to accomplish. To make matters worse, there was nothing I could do about it and certainly no possibility of changing it—I had already tried everything I knew to do, but had failed to prevent the outcome I dreaded most.

> Never underestimate the awesome encouragement you can be to another person or the example you set as a follower of Jesus during the difficult times of your life.

During that time, the Lord showed me very clearly that there was only one way I could face the battle, and that was on my knees. So I went to the prayer room and stayed there until I could honestly say, "Father, not my will, but Your will be done. I submit to Your perfect plan." Doing so did not mean the adversity stopped hurting. It continued to be very painful, more profoundly heartbreaking than anything else I've experienced in my life.

But to my complete surprise, instead of destroying me, this terrible trial flung the doors of ministry open in a manner I never could have imagined. People who hadn't listened to me before—especially non-Christians—began coming up to me, saying, "For a long time I couldn't watch your program because I thought you couldn't possibly understand my suffering and loneliness. I used to think, *What does that man know about all the hurt, pain, and fear I'm facing?* But now—now

I know you appreciate how I feel because you've been there, too. And you've helped me a lot."

God turned the worst heartache of my life into an opportunity to get the gospel to a whole new audience of people throughout the world who desperately needed to hear His message of hope in the midst of their darkness and suffering. The Father can and will do the same in your life if you'll trust Him in it.

The fifth and final reason the Lord allows you to face the pain of dark times is to change your perspective.

Do you recall the dreams Joseph had? This young Hebrew man basically envisioned that one day his brothers would bow to him (Gen. 37:5–11). Of course, as a seventeen-year-old boy, he probably believed that this dream was confirmation that someday he would prove himself to his family and be given the honor he felt he was due. His focus was set on his own validation, plans, and glory.

However, by the time Joseph's brothers traveled to Egypt looking for food, everything had changed (Gen. 42:1–3). Standing before them as the prime minister of Egypt, Joseph's view of life and authority was very different. He understood the astounding responsibility of his office and his accountability before God. He had learned the importance of forgiveness and mercy. And he realized that it was only because of the Lord's great grace that he was in the position to help his family when they needed it most.

Joseph himself communicated this to his brothers by saying, "Do not be grieved or angry with yourselves, because you sold me here, for God sent me before you to preserve life . . . and to keep you alive by a great deliverance. Now, therefore, it was not you who sent me here, but God; and He has made me a father to Pharaoh and lord of all his household and ruler over all the land of Egypt" (Gen. 45:5, 7–8). Joseph recognized that it was the Lord who had engineered it all—even the dark and painful years—for the exceedingly greater purpose of saving many lives.

Like Joseph, you may have people in your life who have treated you cruelly, have taken advantage of you, and have accused you unjustly. But here is what you must remember in every instance: It does you absolutely no good to focus on them, constantly replaying their actions in your mind, which only produces bitterness, anger, and resentment.

Rather, if you are to endure courageously, the way you think about the events of your life needs to change. Like Joseph, you must center your attention on the fact that ultimately, the Lord is the One responsible for your future and all that affects it. Or, as Joseph explained it, "You meant evil against me, but God meant it for good in order to bring about this present result, to preserve many people alive" (Gen. 50:20).

> If you are to endure courageously, you must center your attention on the fact that the Lord is the One responsible for your future and all that affects it.

In other words, the Lord allowed those negative circumstances to touch you because they provided an opportunity for Him to position you for greater blessing and to glorify Himself. If you always keep that in the forefront of your mind, you will be absolutely astonished at all the Father teaches you and accomplishes through you in the course of your trials.

FIGHT THE DARKNESS WITH THE LIGHT OF GOD'S WORD

So far, we have discussed that the way for you to face times of waiting with courage is to remember first that God is with you and second that He has an important purpose for all you're experiencing. However, there is a third principle that is crucial if you wish to endure this difficult season victoriously—and that is to realize that you are in a spiritual battle. In Ephesians 6:12, the apostle Paul affirms, "Our struggle is not against flesh and blood, but against the rulers, against the powers, against the world forces of this darkness, against the spiritual forces of wickedness in the heavenly places." That is, the reason the disheartenment strikes so deep within you is because there is a dangerous enemy striking at the very core of your personhood. How does he do so? Through what you think and believe (2 Cor. 10:4–5).

I can recall experiencing one of the enemy's spiritual attacks as a pastor at my first church, Fruitland Baptist, just outside Hendersonville, North Carolina. I had just graduated from seminary, and I poured my heart into developing my messages—I studied and prayed over every sermon as if it were the only one I would ever preach. Of course, we only had a handful of members in those days, and during those cold North Carolina winters, even fewer people would show up to the services than usual. So when I would stand behind the pulpit and see those empty pews, the devil would take the opportunity to dishearten me, "Look at that. What a waste of time—all that preparation and nobody's here. It appears that no one wants to hear you preach. Well, what did you expect, anyway? God can't use you." Discouraging thoughts kept rushing into my mind, and I knew they weren't from the Father.

So I would pray and God's still small voice would comfort me, "Charles, this isn't all there is. You do your best every Sunday. Study diligently and seek My face for every sermon. Just wait upon Me, trust Me, and see what happens." Don't you know, that's just what I did. And I can truthfully and gratefully say that He has done vastly more on my behalf than I could have ever dreamed.

However, what is important for you to recognize is that the enemy will attempt to discourage you as well. And, friend, there is no more effective time for him to torment you than when you are waiting on God. I warn you of this because it is so easy to believe him and lose heart. His attacks are especially brutal. He knows exactly how to pinpoint the most painful, vulnerable places in your life: the areas of fear, insecurity, rejection, anger, bitterness, pride, and guilt that so readily lead you to despair.

Thankfully, Jesus showed us how to guard ourselves against the enemy's attacks in Matthew 4. He did not argue with the devil, defend Himself, or engage in a discussion. Rather, the Savior confronted Satan's lies with the truth of Scripture.

- When the tempter said, "If You are the Son of God, command that these stones become bread" (v. 3), he was enticing Christ to misuse His power for selfish purposes.

  But Jesus quoted Deuteronomy 8:3, "It is written, 'Man shall not live on bread alone, but on every word that proceeds out of the mouth of God' " (v. 4).

- When the devil had the Savior stand on the pinnacle of the temple, and said to Him, "If You are the Son of God, throw Yourself down" (v. 5), he was trying to persuade Christ to attract followers by performing sensational miracles.

  But Jesus cited Deuteronomy 6:16, "You shall not put the Lord your God to the test" (v. 7).

- And when Satan showed Christ all the kingdoms of the world and said, "All these things I will give You, if You fall down and worship me" (vv. 8–9), he was tempting the Savior to circumvent the crucifixion.

  But Jesus repelled his attack by stating Deuteronomy 6:13, "You shall worship the Lord your God, and serve Him only" (v. 10).

Jesus was victorious against the adversary, and you can be as well. You can resist the devil's disheartening lies with the powerful truth of Scripture. For example:

- When the enemy says, "God has forgotten you," remember that the Lord assures, "I will not forget you" (Isa. 49:15).
- When the adversary accuses, "You've waited so long—you're wasting precious time," recall that Scripture guarantees, "My times are in [the Lord's] hand" (Ps. 31:15).
- When the devil tries to deceive you, stating, "You're going to miss your window of opportunity!" take comfort in the promise, "God . . . acts in behalf of the one who waits for Him" (Isa. 64:4).
- When the evil one threatens, "Everyone will ridicule, despise, and mock you," call to mind the Father's assurance, "Humble yourselves

under the mighty hand of God, that He may exalt you at the proper time" (1 Pet. 5:6).

- When the accuser whispers, "You know you're not really good (attractive, smart, skillful, worthy, or competent, etc.) enough for the blessing," remember that your Defender has promised, "Not by might nor by power, but by My Spirit" (Zech. 4:6).

- When Satan pressures you to waver by saying, "That peace you feel is a lie. God isn't helping you—you're going to fail," strengthen yourself with the biblical truth, "The Lord will accomplish what concerns me; Your loving kindness, O Lord, is everlasting" (Ps. 138:8).

- When the enemy sneers, "You heard the Lord wrong. You don't know His will," hold tightly to the Word, which affirms, "It is God who is at work in you, both to will and to work for His good pleasure" (Phil. 2:13).

- When the adversary taunts, "This is happening because you're useless—no one wants you," recall that the Almighty has proclaimed, "Do not fear, for I have redeemed you; I have called you by name; you are Mine!" (Isa. 43:1).

- When the devil tries to undermine your confidence by jeering, "You've messed up! You've been faithless. Why would the Lord help you?" declare the Savior's promise out loud, "If we are faithless, He remains faithful, for He cannot deny Himself" (2 Tim. 2:13).

- And when the accuser lies to you, saying, "God has abandoned you," remember the vow made by your wonderful, steadfast Deliverer, "The Lord is the one who goes ahead of you; He will be with you. He will not fail you or forsake you. Do not fear or be dismayed" (Deut. 31:8).

Friend, you will spare yourself untold heartache if you realize the negative thoughts that dishearten you are the fiery darts of a spiritual attack and that you can stop them with Scripture. God's Word is your principle weapon in enduring the dark moments of your life coura-geously and triumphantly (Eph. 6:16–17).

Likewise, remember that the enemy will attack you with great dis-couragement and despair before the Lord moves in a great way. Why? Because the adversary wants to steal God's glory and undermine your effectiveness for His kingdom. The evil one's goal is for you to be so discouraged that you question the Father's provision and character. Then, when the Lord answers your prayer, you will feel shame at questioning Him rather than experiencing the wonderful joy of faith made sight. Do not give in to the enemy's tactics.

Instead, "Demolish arguments and every pretension that sets itself up against the knowledge of God, and . . . take captive every thought to make it obedient to Christ" (2 Cor. 10:5). How do you do so? By praying and reading Scripture.

> You will spare yourself untold heartache if you realize the negative thoughts that dishearten you are the fiery darts of a spiritual attack and that you can stop them with Scripture.

Therefore, get on your knees and open the Word of God. Allow the Bible's timeless principles to sink in, to shape your deliberations, and to transform your life. Invite the Holy Spirit to teach you to think as He does and to lead, counsel, and strengthen you. One by one, the Lord will identify the enemy's lies and show you how to overcome them with His truth (John 8:32). Surely, He will guide you, guard you, and encourage you as you hide His Word in your heart.

EXPRESS YOUR COURAGE BY PRAISING HIM

The final principle for remaining courageous during dark times of waiting is found in 1 Thessalonians 5:18, "In everything give thanks; for this is God's will for you in Christ Jesus." That is, on the basis of your relationship with the Savior, you express your appreciation to Him regardless of what happens.

Of course, you may imagine this to be an extremely difficult command, especially during those seasons when the stressors overwhelm you, your dreams are shattered, all seems lost, and you struggle just to get out of bed in the morning. In fact, it seems absolutely counterintuitive to give thanks to the Father in the midst of pain, disappointment, failure, and heartache. Everything in your earthly nature may fight against doing so. But there is a reason that Scripture admonishes you to praise God in *every* situation without exception—not only when life is joyful or easy, but also when your soul most desperately needs hope. And that is because nothing in the world ministers to your spirit or will lift your heart like praising God.

Psalm 92:1–2 declares, "It is good to give thanks to the LORD and to sing praises to Your name, O Most High; to declare Your lovingkindness in the morning and Your faithfulness by night." Why is this? Verse 4 reveals the reason: "For You, O LORD, have made me glad by what You have done, I will sing for joy at the works of Your hands." In other words, when you express your gratefulness to Him, your perspective changes. Instead of continuously mulling over the negative aspects of your life, you actively look for His help and deliverance, which have never failed you.

I've said it many times throughout this book: There is absolutely nothing more important than keeping your focus on God rather than dwelling on your circumstances. Giving thanks to Him throughout this season—especially in the darkest moments—helps you do just that. This is because as you look for reasons to praise Him, you find yourself more:

- Aware of His presence and all the ways He is moving in your situation,
- Motivated to look for His purpose in every detail and consider the ways He is preparing you for greater blessings,
- Sensitive to what the Holy Spirit is teaching you,

- Dependent upon Him for every aspect of your life,
- Cognizant of the wisdom of the Father's plan,
- And surrendered to His will.

For example, earlier in this chapter I mentioned one of the most excruciating trials I have ever experienced, when I thought I would lose everything, including my ministry. During that time, I took this command to thank Him very seriously and set my heart to be grateful. The trial was so devastating that, at first, I struggled to find reasons to give Him thanks. So I began with my relationship with the Savior. I expressed my appreciation for all Jesus had done on the Cross: forgiving my sins, reconciling me to the Father, adopting me into His family, filling me with His Holy Spirit, giving me a new nature, and providing me with eternal life and a home in heaven.

This led me to more areas of gratefulness. I thanked Him for being the unfailing God of all creation—the omnipotent, omniscient, omnipresent, and loving King of kings and Lord of lords, who is perfect in all His ways. I acknowledged that though some people had deserted me, He had blessed me with many loving family members and friends who were steadfast in their support. I recognized that He had not failed to provide for me or encourage me through His Word. I praised Him for the promises He had given me, for strengthening my faith, for refining my character, for all the ways He had proven Himself faithful to me in the past, and for being in control of every aspect of my life.

Before I knew it, I was thanking the Father for the trial itself—that it was not a surprise to Him. Though I did not understand it all, I acknowledged that He had allowed it for His higher purposes and that because of the assurance of Romans 8:28, I could count on Him to bring something good from it. I also recognized that the greater the hurt I experienced, the closer I grew to Him, so I expressed my gratefulness that He was drawing me into a more profoundly intimate relationship. I admitted that the difficulty had revealed areas in my life that were not fully submitted to Him, and I expressed my appreciation that He was ridding me of strongholds. Likewise, I was glad to have a better understanding of the deep pain others feel so that I could be a better encourager, comforter, and minister of the gospel.

As I continued, my reasons to worship the Lord increased. Every moment, the Father brought new areas of gratefulness to mind and it absolutely restored my soul.

Praise God in the midst of these difficult circumstances and receive His encouragement and energy to persevere.

Friend, you can do the same. You can praise God in the midst of these difficult circumstances and receive His encouragement and energy to persevere. You can thank Him that through these dark times, He is conforming you to the likeness of Christ, molding your character to reflect His (Rom. 8:29). You can express your gratefulness that He is teaching you to think as He thinks; love in the unconditional manner He loves; and forgive freely the way He forgives you. Because when you do, it honors the Lord greatly, refreshes your spirit, and helps you to endure courageously and victoriously.

Therefore, ask yourself:

- In this situation, what can I thank Him for? What good could the Lord possibly bring from this trial?
- How is the Lord making me aware of His presence and activity in my life?
- What has the Father taught me about Himself during this season? How is our relationship growing stronger?
- What purpose is the Lord revealing to me in the details of my life? How is God preparing me through this trial for greater blessings?
- What has the Holy Spirit been teaching me through my time in prayer, in His Word, and as I fellowship with other believers?
- How am I becoming more dependent upon God through this difficulty, and how is He setting me free from sin?

•✓ Finally, how is the Father helping me to surrender to His will
through this trial?

As you answer those questions, you will certainly find abundant reasons to thank Him. Likewise, as you make praise a part of your times alone with Him, I challenge you to make it an integral part of your public life as well. Declare your gratefulness to Him and confidence in Him as you talk to others about what He is doing in your life.

If instead of declaring our gratefulness and confidence in God to others we are negative about our circumstances, we will not only discourage ourselves further through our complaining, but we also dishearten our listeners. This doesn't help anyone. But when you publicly express your trust that God will help you, not only does it strengthen your own soul, it also blesses whoever hears you and spurs them on to trust the Father more (Col. 3:16–17; Heb. 10:24).

TOWARD THE LIGHT

The truth of the matter is, all of us have walked through valleys at one time in life or another. Each of us has wept over prolonged difficulties and struggles that we thought we couldn't survive. We lay awake at night, wondering, *God, what am I going to do? I don't know how to go on.* We're not sure how to face the decisions and consequences that will come. The pain and emptiness overwhelm us.

But friend, take courage in the fact that there is a limit to your suffering, and the dark moments of your life will continue only as long as is necessary for God to accomplish His purposes in you (Ps. 138:8). As Psalm 30:5 says, "Weeping may last for the night, but a shout of joy comes in the morning." This time of adversity is difficult, but it won't endure forever. Stay on course with Him, and soon enough you will walk in the light of His love.

Nothing illustrated this to me so powerfully as when I took a flight across the Atlantic a few years back. The pilot explained that our night would be shortened because we were flying east—soaring directly toward the dawn. Sitting there in the darkness, I kept looking out the window to see if I could see any sign of the rising sun. Finally, my eye caught a glimpse of a tiny sliver of light on the horizon. It wasn't much, but because I knew where to look, I saw that morning was only minutes away.

That is the way it is for us as believers. Yes, we may go through some very dark moments in life. But our heavenly Father is moving us toward the light on the most efficient and effective route possible. If we keep our focus and our bearing set on Him, the night will be shortened. But if we veer from the course He has set, we will only lengthen our time of darkness.

> Our heavenly Father is moving us toward the light on the most efficient and effective route possible.

Therefore, the way you respond is extremely important. So no matter what happens or how discouraging your situation may become, never stop clinging to the Father. It is absolutely crucial that you remain courageous and continue to trust God through this time, rejoicing in His presence with you, resting in His plan, claiming His promises, and praising His name. Because if you rebel against Him in the dark moments, all you're doing is prolonging the time of the adversity.

But if you will remain faithful as Joseph did and trust God to guide you through this difficult season of your life, then the Lord will do amazing things in and through you. He will move you from the prison of despair to the wonderful place of all His fulfilled promises. And that, friend, is certainly worth staying on track for, no matter how dark the night may become.

Father, how grateful I am that You are my God through darkness and light, adversity and blessing. Thank You, Lord, for being so gracious and compassionate toward me—for taking care of me when I feel so weak and powerless. I confess the delays wear on my soul and the obstacles can become overwhelming. But I know You never give me more than I can handle and only allow the trials that will strengthen my faith, build my character, and deepen my relationship with You.

Therefore, Father, I declare my confidence in You. I thank You for Your constant presence with me throughout the difficult seasons. You are my hope and my adequacy. I trust Your purposes—that through these challenges, You are preparing me for Your wonderful plans for my life. Thank You for perfecting my faith, making me a testimony of Your love and provision, influencing others through me, and teaching me to see my circumstances from Your perspective.

Father, help me to discern when the negative thoughts I have are a spiritual attack, and lead me to verses in Your Word that I can call upon as a defense. I also pray that You will always help me to praise You—for rightly You are worthy of all honor and glory. Truly, it is good to give You thanks and declare Your loving-kindness. May I always be a faithful witness of Your unwavering goodness and grace.

Lord, You have given me hope and purpose when they were lost to me. Thank You for helping me endure this dark season of delay. Keep me on course in the perfect path of Your will so that I may very soon walk in the light of Your fulfilled promises. In the holy, unfailing name of Jesus I pray. Amen.

POINTS FOR ACTIVE WAITING

1. Memorize Deuteronomy 31:6, "Be strong and courageous, do not be afraid or tremble at them, for the LORD your God is the one who goes with you. He will not fail you or forsake you."

2. Whenever you feel anxious because of this season of delay, repeat Deuteronomy 31:6, Hebrews 10:23, Philippians 2:13, Proverbs 3:5–6, Psalm 62:5–6, and Psalm 27:14 to yourself.

3. As you pray today, consider the adversity you are facing at the moment and ask God to help you answer the following questions. Write what you learn in the space provided or in your journal.

    a. Would you say you have little faith, maturing faith, or perfect faith? How is God working through this dark season to prove or strengthen your trust in Him?

    b. In what ways can you see the Lord preparing you? What aspects of your character does it appear He is developing?

    c. Is the Father calling you to serve Him by blessing others? In what way?

4. Review the ways the enemy attacks you beginning on page 181. Which negative thoughts stand out to you the most? Which Scripture passages are most meaningful? For your own defense, consider memorizing those verses and repeat them to yourself often.

5. Remember to thank God daily and praise Him for faithfully accomplishing all that concerns you. If you need help doing so during this time, refer to the questions that begin on page 186.

Use this space to respond to the "Points for Active Waiting" and to record prayer requests, key lessons God is teaching you, and your insights about waiting on the Lord to act on your behalf.

From days of old
they have not heard or perceived by ear,
nor has the eye seen a God besides You,
Who acts in behalf of the one who waits for Him.
—Isaiah 64:4

7

THE JOY OF WAITING

Reaping the Rewards

I love photographing eagles. Not only are they beautiful, but they are also extremely interesting to watch. These powerful, intense birds can ascend to an altitude of more than ten thousand feet, fly level at speeds of thirty-five mph, dive at more than seventy-five mph, and see more than three miles away. They are absolutely amazing. Thankfully, throughout my life, God has given me several opportunities to capture wonderful images of their majestic flight—as they effortlessly glide through the air, circle with strength and accuracy, pick up fish with their mighty talons, and soar away. It is truly exciting and awe-inspiring to observe them.

But what I love best about these regal creatures is that they remind me of the awesome truth of Isaiah 40:30–31, "Though youths grow weary and tired, and vigorous young men stumble badly, those who wait for the LORD will gain new strength; they will mount up with wings like eagles, they will run and not get tired, they will walk and not become weary." Isaiah could not have chosen anything more picturesque or appropriate to express the profound promise of waiting on God.

Why? Because of the wonderful way the Father has created these majestic birds to traverse the firmament. Eagles rarely bat their strong wings when they are airborne. They instinctively understand that if they rely on their own power to stay aloft, they would tire quickly and wouldn't be able to travel very far. So instead they wait, find the right air current to support them, and move effortlessly through the sky by the force of the wind stream that carries them. Then, because of the amazing vision the Lord has given them, they can tell the difference between a rockfish and a salmon from a great distance, and will only alight when their preferred quarry is in view.

What a beautiful application of the Christian life. The wind current that carries us through every trial and time of delay is our trust in God.

When we strive, struggle, and impulsively attempt to achieve our goals without Him, we grow tired—weary of life and hopeless to the depths of our soul. Perhaps you have experienced this feeling of utter internal exhaustion—the intense realization that life cannot continue on as is. It leads to a discouragement and despair that are so difficult to overcome.

But this is the promise our heavenly Father has given us: When we wait upon Him, He will renew our strength by becoming the powerful force beneath our wings—lifting us to new heights, supporting us in the journey, and taking us to our desired haven. He enables us to fly high above the problems or trials we face. He makes us mighty like the eagles—with a strong vision that is wisely able to discern the Lord's will from any harmful desire that we may have. And so, from the eagles we learn that the wonderful plans God has for us will come to fruition when we wait for the mighty wind of His Spirit to support and empower us, moving us through His provision to the right destination.

> When we wait upon God, He will become the powerful current beneath our wings—lifting us to new heights, supporting us in the journey, and taking us to our desired haven.

THE REWARDS OF WAITING

Friend, concerning that deep desire of your heart—you may still be tempted to make it happen. Even as you finish this book about waiting on God, you may be filled with a sense of restlessness. This is not uncommon, because this struggle has no easy solution. Rather, it requires a day-by-day—sometimes moment-by-moment—determination to trust the Father. With this determination, you actively resist the temptation to make your own way or accept less than the Lord's very best, because you realize that doing so would mean throwing away your life.

Likewise, your willingness to wait for your heart's desire reveals the value you place on the object you are waiting for. If you truly cherish it—if you really respect and honor the Father—then you will exhibit patience, faith, and obedience as you endure expectantly and wait for Him to act. You will wait for the Lord, confidently anticipating that when the right moment comes, He will lift you—as if soaring on wings like eagles—and take you where you should go.

Of course, it is much easier to wait when you know the rewards of doing so. Lamentations 3:25 promises, "The LORD is good to those who wait for Him, to the person who seeks Him." So how does the Father bless you when you trust in His provision? How does He lift you up, alleviate your weariness, and give you the strength to continue?

First, as we discussed previously, God does so by revealing His will for your life and for what concerns you.

God will show you what to do, guide you in making wise decisions, and give you discernment about the opportunities ahead of you. You don't have to wear yourself out fretting about your situation. Rather, Psalm 37:34 (TLB) promises, "Keep traveling steadily along his pathway"—however the Father directs you to go—"and in due season he will honor you with every blessing."

Do you realize the freedom in this? You do not have to control your circumstances, wrestle with confusion, or worry about every contingency. You simply have to make the determination that the Lord is God, remain in close fellowship with Him, and obey Him. And you can do this with great confidence because He will always enable you to do anything He calls you to accomplish. You are guaranteed that you will be successful as you follow His leadership (Ps. 37:4–6).

Second, the Lord gives you supernatural energy, wisdom, and strength.

You will be able to keep on going when other people fall by the wayside. Why? Because by waiting on God, you accept that He is the One who empowers and carries you. Like the eagle, you don't have to bat your wings or struggle, because the wind current of the Father's unfailing provision carries you.

Sadly, when you don't wait, just the opposite is true. A simple illustration of this would be trying to change a flat tire on your automobile without any tools. If you attempted to lift the car with one hand and then expected to remove the tire with the other, you would certainly find your goal absolutely impossible. You would most likely exhaust and injure yourself in the process, but still not get anywhere. But employ a jack and other useful tools, and the whole situation changes.

We act just as foolishly when we fail to wait on God and try to manage spiritual matters—like charting a course for our future—without the wisdom and guidance of the Holy Spirit. In fact, you and I are more likely to succeed in lifting a big rig truck with one finger than we are in handling the supernatural trials that assail us. Remember, "Our struggle is not against flesh and blood, but against the rulers, against the powers, against the world forces of this darkness, against the spiritual forces of wickedness in the heavenly places" (Eph. 6:12). If we insist on fighting these battles with our own strength, we will wear ourselves out and make no progress.

But when you rely on God—when He is your energy and might—He empowers you, giving you resources that vastly surpass your human capabilities and that defy explanation. Isaiah 40:28–29 promises, "The

Everlasting God, the LORD, the Creator of the ends of the earth does not become weary or tired. His understanding is inscrutable. He gives strength to the weary, and to him who lacks might He increases power." It is absolutely astonishing what the Father can and will accomplish through you when you willingly wait for Him.

Finally, God will answer your prayers, and you will see the fulfillment of your faith.

The Father affirms in Isaiah 49:23, "I am the LORD; those who hopefully wait for Me will not be put to shame." When you wait on God, you never have to worry that your life won't work out right or that your trust in Him is in vain. You can have full confidence that the best is ahead because almighty God Himself guarantees it.

But when you rely on God, He gives you resources that vastly surpass your human capabilities and that defy explanation.

You see, when you embrace the Father's schedule and truly trust Him, He will provide what you long for most in a way that is even better than you can imagine and which transforms you in the very depths of your soul.

Remember the promise of Isaiah 64:4? "From days of old they have not heard or perceived by ear, nor has the eye seen a God besides You, Who acts in behalf of the one who waits for Him." Think about that. The eternal, unfailing King of kings is working everything out for you! Your loving heavenly Father is engineering the finest, most effective answers to your dearest prayers. All of the resources of heaven are marshaled in your best interest. All circumstances, events, and details are arranged with the Lord's great plan for you in view.

Additionally, as He answers your prayer, the Father gives you a sense of everlasting purpose and importance in the moments of your life. You realize that not only were His wonderful gifts planned for you before your birth, but before the very foundation of the world (Eph. 1). And they won't come and go quickly like earthly achievements or rewards; rather, He will carry them on to completion in eternity—they will continue blessing you and others until the day of Christ Jesus (Phil. 1:6). And best of all, you get to know Him better through all of it. What an awesome God we serve!

A LASTING INVESTMENT

Friend, God is most certainly working on your behalf, even though His wonderful plans for you take time. And my prayer for you is that you would learn to anticipate His answer—no matter how long it takes—and to do so faithfully, patiently, and joyfully. You have invested so much time, energy, prayer, and confidence into waiting for Him that it would be a shame for you to abandon your hope now—when you are on the brink of blessing and when His answer for you is closer than ever before. So don't give up. Do not ever give up.

Be assured He is actively, powerfully, wisely, and lovingly arranging the circumstances of your life. As I've assured you throughout the pages of this book—even though His activity may not be obvious to you—He is drawing you closer, refining your character, teaching you His ways, and fulfilling His promises to you.

First Corinthians 2:9–10, 12 teaches, " 'Eye has not seen and ear has not heard . . . all that God has prepared for those who love him.' For to us God revealed them through the Spirit . . . So that we may know the things freely given to us by God." In other words, you may not be able to imagine all that the Father is doing in and through the days, months, and years you have been seeking Him, but it is absolutely awesome. And if you wait for Him with expectant endurance—directing your focus to Him, purposefully seeking His will through Scripture and prayer, actively claiming His promises, and courageously facing adversity with faith—you will certainly see the fruit of your obedience. While you expectantly wait, here's what you can do:

First, humble yourself before the Lord and focus on Him rather than your desire.

Agree with the Father that He is right about His timing, His plan, and even about any sin He has revealed in your life. Remember He is the omniscient, omnipotent, omnipresent, unconditionally loving God who will never fail you. You can depend upon Him to help you no matter what happens.

Second, remain obedient to God's will.

Find purpose for your life by pursuing and submitting to the Lord's perfect direction, preparation, and provision. Read His Word, pray, seek godly counsel, and pay attention to the Holy Spirit as He speaks through the circumstances of your life. Allow Him to guide you step-by-step because He will never steer you wrong.

Third, have faith that the Father will do as He has promised.

Every day, actively express your trust that God will keep His Word to you (1 Kings 8:56). You can wholeheartedly count on the Lord because He has never once failed and never will. He will *always* fulfill His promises to you.

Finally, be courageous.

God is accomplishing important purposes during this time of waiting—even when your situation appears completely hopeless. So set your heart steadfastly on Him—even when the winds of adversity, persecution, and disappointment assail you—confident that He is bringing good from your situation and drawing you ever closer to your reward.

ENDURE EXPECTANTLY—ALWAYS

We began this journey with a list of "nevers." However, I pray that after reading these pages, you've been encouraged and have discovered principles and biblical truths that will strengthen you whenever the Father appears to delay and human reason tells you to give up.

You can and should endure expectantly with the joy of knowing God will never let you down. You can and should keep hoping even when the *nevers* of life bombard you, realizing that the Lord is the One you really hope for, and He perfectly cares for all that concerns you. You can trust the Father to lead you and know for absolute certain that He has your very best interests in mind.

> The word *always* beautifully describes how committed God is to you and to your well-being.

We've come a long way from the *nevers*. And with that in mind, I want to end with a far more optimistic theme—a word that I hope you'll remember when you wait on the Lord. A word that applies to His wonderful, unfailing character. A word that beautifully describes how committed He is to you and to your well-being.

Always.

As a believer:

God will *always* be with you.

He will *always* accept you.

He will *always* love you.

He will *always* claim you as His own.

He will *always* listen to you.

He will *always* comfort you.

He will *always* provide for you.

He will *always* forgive your sins.

He will *always* remember you.

He will *always* work on your behalf.

He will *always* lead you with love, power, and wisdom.

He will *always* bless your obedience.

He will *always* come through for you.

He will *always* answer your prayers.

And when you wait on the Lord, you can know for certain that the best is yet to come . . . *always.*

Father, You are truly the undeniable, everlasting, omnipotent, omniscient, omnipresent, and unconditionally loving God—the Lord, the Creator of the ends of the earth. You do not become tired or weary, Your understanding and wisdom are unfathomable. How grateful I am that as I wait upon You, You help me mount up with wings like an eagle's. You reveal Your will to me, fill me with Your supernatural energy and strength, answer my prayers in ways more wonderful than I can imagine, and fill me with an understanding of Your eternal purposes.

Father, I confess that my soul continues to become restless—I am still tempted to take matters into my own hands or settle for less than Your best. But Lord God, I choose You. Right now I affirm that I want You—Your will and Your ways—above all else. Please keep me on Your track for my life—in the center of Your perfect plans and purposes that You envisioned for me even before I existed.

I thank You for this time of waiting, Father. I thank You for all You've taught me and all You are teaching me still. I thank You for drawing me closer to You, refining my character, preparing me for Your answer to my prayers, redeeming my time, sustaining me when I am too weary to go on, renewing my strength, and fulfilling Your promises. And I praise You, Father, for always being with me, accepting me, loving me, claiming me as Your own, listening to me, comforting me, providing for me, forgiving me of my sins, remembering me, working on my behalf, leading me, blessing my obedience, coming through for me, answering my prayers, and always giving me hope that the best is yet to come. To You, my precious Lord, I dedicate my life and all that is ahead. I wait in hope for You.

In the matchless, wonderful, holy name of Jesus I pray. Amen.

POINTS FOR ACTIVE WAITING

1. Memorize Isaiah 64:4, "From days of old they have not heard or perceived by ear, Nor has the eye seen a God besides You, Who acts in behalf of the one who waits for Him."
2. Whenever you feel anxious because of this season of delay, repeat Isaiah 64:4, Deuteronomy 31:6, Hebrews 10:23, Philippians 2:13, Proverbs 3:5–6, Psalm 62:5–6, and Psalm 27:14 to yourself.
3. Whenever you grow discouraged, remember to thank God for His activity in the unseen (Isa. 64:4). Review the notes you've taken as you've read this book and all the ways the Father has spoken to you. Thank Him for all He's taught you and praise Him daily for faithfully accomplishing all that concerns you.

Use this space to record how God has answered your prayers thus far, along with the requests you are still waiting for. Likewise, record the key lessons God has taught you, the ways you have drawn closer to Him, and how He has changed your life as you've waited on Him.

_____

_____

_____

_____

_____

_____

_____

_____

_____

_____

_____

_____

_____

_____

_____

_____

_____

_____

_____

_____

_____

_____

_____

NOTES

CHAPTER 1

1 Don Richardson, *Eternity in Their Hearts: Startling Evidence of Belief in the One True God* (Ventura, CA: Regal Books, 2006), 87.

2 Hal Seed, *The Bible Questions: Shedding Light on the World's Most Important Book* (Downers Grove, IL: InterVarsity Press, 2012), 48.

3 Richardson, *Eternity in Their Hearts*, 87.

4 The Solar Probe Plus—NASA's ambitious and impressive effort to examine the sun's atmosphere—will reach within 3.8 million miles of its surface. It is set to launch in 2018. http://www.jhuapl.edu /newscenter/pressreleases/2014/140318.asp.

5 This phrase was originally penned by Algernon Sydney, and was later quoted by Ben Franklin in his work, *Poor Richard's Almanack*.

CHAPTER 5

1 Andrew Murray, *Waiting on God* (New York: Fleming H. Revell Co., 1896), 61.

CHAPTER 6

6 Bob McEowen, "Hamilton's favorite son," Rural Missouri, http://www.ruralmissouri.org/08pages/08MayJCPenney.html.

7   Victor M. Parachin, "The hymn that brought J.C. Penney to
    salvation," LifeWay, http://www.lifeway.com/Article/mature
    -living-the-hymn-that-brought-JC-Penney-to-salvation.

8   Civilla Durfee Martin, 1904, http://cyberhymnal.org/htm/g/w
    /gwiltake.htm.

9   Albert Benjamin Simpson, *Days of Heaven Upon Earth* (Nyack,
    N.Y.: Christian Alliance Publishing Co., 1897) 222.